"I have always loved Dr. Moseley, as a teacher, for his clarity. While it is obvious he has done his research in preparing this study, he writes so that ordinary people can apply Solomon's wisdom in a way that will transform their lives. Textually faithful, gospel-rich, and well-organized, this is a go-to resource for understanding the great Book of wisdom."

—J.D. GREEAR, pastor, The Summit Church
(Raleigh-Durham, North Carolina);
author, *Gaining by Losing: Why the Future Belongs to Churches that Send*

"Proverbs 23:23 instructs us to 'buy truth, and do not sell it.' Allan Moseley in this book provides illustrations, explanation, and questions to allow the reader to encounter the book of Wisdom in a new and fresh way. Anyone desiring to live wisely should read this book, which will guide you in truth for living a godly life."

—THOMAS WHITE, president, Cedarville University

"I've always had a hard time getting a handle on how to preach and teach from the book of Proverbs. Because the book jumps quickly from one subject to another, and then repeatedly revisits many of its subjects, synthesizing the material can be a big challenge. That's one of the reasons I'm so thankful for Dr. Allan Moseley's *Living Well*. As a Hebrew scholar, he expertly draws together the various strands of truth in Proverbs to show the overarching teaching of the book on subjects such as relationships, speech, anger, pride, money, and wisdom itself. Even more, as a master Bible teacher, he illustrates and applies the truth he presents with precision and insight. Most significantly, he connects the wisdom of Proverbs to God's ultimate wisdom, Jesus Christ. *Living Well* is a transformative book. For years to come, it will be a go-to resource any time I study Proverbs."

—STEPHEN N. RUMMAGE, pastor,
Bell Shoals Baptist Church (Brandon, Florida)

"Over the years, Proverbs has become one of my favorite books in the Bible. Proverbs is filled with principles that help cultivate godly wisdom and contribute to human flourishing. They also point to Jesus Christ, 'who became wisdom from God for us—our righteousness, sanctification, and redemption' (1 Cor 1:30 CSB). In *Living Well*, Allan Moseley opens up the Proverbs and brings them to bear on ten different aspects of the Christian life. This delightful book is blessed with the insights of an Old Testament scholar, the illustrations and applications of a skilled preacher, and the devotional warmth of a mature follower of Jesus Christ. It will prove helpful to preachers and teachers of God's Word, will make a wonderful supplement to personal devotional reading in the Proverbs, and will serve as a great resource for study groups. Highly recommended."

—NATHAN A. FINN, dean of the School of Theology and Missions and
professor of theological studies, Union University

"This book is vintage Allan Moseley! It is biblical, clear, practical, and witty. It perfectly represents the genre of Proverbs. The Proverbs were intended for real life. Moseley masterfully puts this on full display in this very fine work."

—Dr. Daniel L. Akin, president,
Southeastern Baptist Theological Seminary

"In our paradoxical world where wrong is increasingly seen as right and where the very notions of what is good and true are fading, how refreshing to be reminded that God gives us the playbook of Proverbs to help us live successful and significant lives. N. Allan Moseley helps us see God's wisdom for relationships, health, money, and life in general in a light that brings to life the deeper meaning of proverbs we have perhaps read many times. *Living Well* will remain on my table, next to my Bible, for those daily encounters when I need another helping of God's promised wisdom."

—Dan Forest, lieutenant governor of North Carolina

LIVING WELL

God's Wisdom from the Book of Proverbs

ALLAN MOSELEY

LEXHAM PRESS

Print ISBN 9781683590101
Digital ISBN 9781683590118

Lexham Editorial: Jennifer Edwards, Rebecca Florence Miller, Abigail Stocker, Lisa Eary, Elizabeth Vince
Cover Design: Christine Christophersen
Back Cover Design: Brittany Schrock
Typesetting: ProjectLuz.com

CONTENTS

PREFACE

IN 2003, A. J. JACOBS PUBLISHED A BOOK ENTITLED *THE KNOW-It-All*. That book was based on his experience of reading through the *Encyclopaedia Britannica* in one year. He read all forty-four million words on thirty-three thousand pages. Mr. Jacobs, a journalist by trade, now knows all sorts of minutiae. He knows that the British tried to tax clocks in 1797, that absentee voting is very popular in Ireland, and that there is a heated controversy over who invented the accordion.

Mr. Jacobs personifies "the information age." We have access to more information than any former generation. However, access to information is not the same as the development of wisdom. Just ask Mr. Jacobs. His vast reservoir of knowledge hardly made him wiser, and he admits that it did not make him smarter. Mainly, it made him annoying to his family. His wife started fining him for every fact he mentioned that wasn't relevant to their conversation.[1]

In contrast with that, God has given us the biblical book of Proverbs to teach us knowledge about life. The information in Proverbs is not for the purpose of filling our heads with facts, but to help us live successful lives. The contents of the book of Proverbs are not up-to-the-minute factoids; they are lessons about living that have endured for three thousand years. Furthermore, they express not merely the opinion or wisdom of people, but God's revelation. At times God's wisdom runs against the wisdom common to human beings. Sometimes it confronts it head on. When it does, it seems radical to us.

What is the worth of God's wisdom? Proverbs 3:13 says, "Blessed is the one who finds wisdom, and the one who gets understanding." The verses that follow describe the great worth of God's wisdom by means of a series of comparisons. First, wisdom is *valuable*. Verse 14 says, "The gain from [Wisdom] is better than gain from silver and her profit better than gold." Verse 15 begins, "She is more precious than jewels." That's an amazing statement. God's wisdom is worth more than silver, gold, and jewels. Solomon, who wrote most of the Proverbs, had plenty of silver, gold, and jewels. He was a rich man. But he wrote here that wisdom is more valuable than all of that.

A second word that expresses the value of wisdom is *incomparable*. The second part of verse 15 says, "Nothing you desire can compare with her." Think of the thing you desire most. Whatever it is, its worth doesn't compare with the worth of God's wisdom.

Third, wisdom is *beneficial*. Verse 16 of Proverbs 3 states the following about wisdom: "Long life is in her right hand; in her left hand are riches and honor." So, if you want long life, riches, and honor, learn God's wisdom. Verse 17 says, "Her ways are ways of pleasantness, and all her paths are peace." The word for peace is *shalom*. That word, usually translated "peace," was used to refer to more than the absence of conflict. It also referred to wholeness and well-being. When we walk in the way of wisdom, we are in a position to receive many benefits that would not be available to us if we lived foolishly. The benefits include a longer life, more wealth, peace with others, and peace within ourselves.

Fourth, wisdom is *powerful*. Proverbs 3:19 says, "The LORD by wisdom founded the earth; by understanding he established the heavens." Using his wisdom, God created the universe. When we go to God to receive his wisdom, we're accessing something that is powerful. If God used his wisdom to create the vast and intricate universe, certainly his wisdom will make a great difference in our lives. Never doubt the worth of God's wisdom.

So, we begin our encounter with the book of Proverbs by emphasizing how valuable the wisdom contained in this book is. Years ago I told God that I wanted to seek his wisdom in the book of Proverbs. I asked him to give me wisdom from his word. So I read through the book of Proverbs slowly, and I categorized every verse according to its subject. I isolated over forty subjects addressed in the book of Proverbs, like interpersonal relationships, handling finances, marriage and parenting, anger, and the use of speech. Through the years, I have returned to that list of verses many times for guidance in my life. Over and over I have read what God's book of wisdom has to say, and it has been an immeasurable help to me.

I wrote this book because my friend Elaine Funderburk suggested that I do so. One of G. K. Chesterton's friends made such a suggestion to him once too. In the resulting book, *Orthodoxy*, he commented, "It was perhaps an incautious suggestion to make to a person only too ready to write books upon the feeblest provocation."[2] When Elaine reads this book I hope she does not conclude that her suggestion was incautious! I am grateful to Lexham Press for their encouragement and help in producing this volume, especially to Jennifer Edwards and Abigail Stocker for their editorial suggestions. I am also grateful to my family for their patience with me as I wrote, sometimes sequestered away while on family vacation. I'm also grateful for Southeastern Baptist Theological

Seminary, where I teach, and the people of Christ Baptist Church, so many of whom live the words of this book.

The themes herein were chosen because of their prominence in Proverbs and their relevance to living in today's world. In the introduction, I attempt to prepare readers to benefit from the book of Proverbs by providing some necessary background information. The balance of the book is divided into three sections. Part 1 pertains to living well in our relationships. In this section, I look at the people skills the book of Proverbs helps us develop and at how our words powerfully affect our relationships. Since so many of our relationships are affected by how we think about masculinity and femininity, we'll also consider God's wisdom about manhood and womanhood. Part 2 pertains to living well within our own hearts, because Proverbs imparts so much wisdom about defeating anger and pride, and developing joy. Work, money, and sex are also major parts of our lives and culture, so in Part 3 I address the wisdom in Proverbs related to those subjects.

I hope that reading this book will result in a continuing journey to seek wisdom as if we were seeking silver or gold. Such a journey will make us a success in the best sense of that word. At times the journey will take us in a radically different direction from those around us. But if we follow the path of God's wisdom we will live well, because we will look at everything in our lives through eyes that have been enlightened by divine wisdom.

INTRODUCING THE BOOK OF PROVERBS

WHEN I WAS IN HIGH SCHOOL, THE YOUTH GROUP IN MY home church went on a mission trip. On the way home, the bus stopped at a mall, and I bought a little book entitled *Poor Richard's Quotations*. The book consisted of quotes from *Poor Richard's Almanac*, edited by Benjamin Franklin. That almanac featured proverbs. When I bought the book, I had no idea how much I would enjoy reading those proverbs, rereading them, and thinking about them through the years. It's been many years since I first read that book (how many years will remain a safely guarded secret), but I often think of those proverbs.

The reason I remember proverbs I read so long ago is that they are so closely related to everyday life. For example, when I'm visiting in someone's home and I face a variety of foods that do not look especially appealing, I remember, "Hunger never saw bad bread." The meaning of the proverb is clear—when we're really hungry, anything will taste good. "Content makes poor men rich; discontent makes rich men poor" has prodded me to remember to be grateful and satisfied with what I have.

And I've always liked "Tomorrow every fault will be amended, but that tomorrow never comes."[1] It's another way of saying, "Don't put off until tomorrow what you can do today." Mark Twain's sarcastic version was "Never put off until tomorrow what you can put off until the day after tomorrow."[2] If *Poor Richard's* proverbs sound good to you, I can guarantee you that the proverbs God inspired are infinitely more valuable. So you made the right choice to dive into this book. When we master the proverbs God gave us, they will help us live well every day of our lives.

A WISER KIND OF WISDOM

When people learn and live according to God's wisdom they will be swimming upstream in a downstream world.[3] Why? Because God's wisdom in the book of Proverbs is immeasurably wiser than what most of the people in the world consider wise. The world says being rich is the way to go! Proverbs says being generous is wise (19:17; 22:9). Western culture encourages us to promote ourselves to get ahead. Proverbs says, "Let another praise you, and not your own mouth" (27:2). Many people live by the rule, "Stay out of other people's business." God's book of wisdom says, "Better is open rebuke than hidden love" (27:5). It's most common for people to think that having lots of money will bring happiness and contentment. Proverbs says, "Whoever trusts in his riches will fall" (11:28).

God's wisdom is not like the wisdom people create. To see that, maybe we should start by defining the Hebrew word translated "wisdom," which is *chokmah*. In the Old Testament, that word is used generally in three ways. First, it refers to the possession of a skill. If you know the names Bezalel and Oholiab, you could probably do well in a game of Bible trivia. Bezalel and Oholiab were two artisans who helped to construct the tabernacle in the wilderness. They were skilled in building things and in working with precious metals. In Exodus 31:6 and elsewhere, Bezalel and Oholiab are said to have *chokmah*, or wisdom. They were wise in that they had a skill, or trade, that enabled them to make a living.

Second, *chokmah* is used to refer to skill in living—not just a life skill to make a living, but skill in living life. That is the way "wisdom" is used in the book of Proverbs. It refers to the ability to live well. In the book of Proverbs, wisdom has to do with knowing how to use words well, how to control anger, how to handle finances well, how to avoid temptation, etc. Those things are wise, and they lead to success in the best sense of that word.

Third, "wisdom" is used to refer to knowing and fearing God. Wisdom books like Job and Ecclesiastes address finding meaning in life, and finding meaning in life is finding God. Job and his friends could not explain the meaning of suffering despite their best efforts. They needed God, and when God showed up, Job found meaning. The writer of Ecclesiastes claimed that all the paths people follow to find happiness are dead ends, and they end in futility. All paths, that is, except for the one path of knowing and fearing God. Proverbs 1:7 and 9:10 say that relating properly to God, specifically fearing God, is the starting point of wisdom. In other words, we have to know God to live well.

Possession of a life skill, living skillfully, and knowing God—those are practical, life-related matters. They affect the way we live every day. God's wisdom is practical, but we should not make the mistake of equating his wisdom with common sense. Common sense is natural, but wisdom is supernatural because it comes from God. The irony is that the world's way of success is actually the way to fail. Though people who follow the world's wisdom may succeed partially and temporarily, they will ultimately fail to become wise, at least in God's eyes. On the other hand, when we give up the world's way of success and seek God's way of wisdom, we live well now, and we live forever.

PROVERBS, GOD, AND
THE GOSPEL OF JESUS CHRIST

The book of Proverbs is more than a repository of "how to" principles for successful living. It is part of the grand narrative of God's past, present, and future work of salvation that is unveiled in Scripture. In many ways, the book of Proverbs demonstrates that wisdom can be accessed only in a relationship with God. Fearing God, or living in a right relationship with Him, is the beginning of wisdom (Prov 1:7; 9:10), and readers of Proverbs are exhorted to "Trust in the LORD with all your heart" (3:5). We cannot have God's wisdom without God, because as Proverbs 2:6 says, "The LORD gives wisdom." In the old covenant period, the Lord gave wisdom to those who put their faith in him and thus became part of the covenant people (Gen 15:6; Gal 3:5–14).

The New Testament also highlights that true wisdom is inextricably bound to relatedness to God. Paul emphasized that the "sacred writings" of the Old Testament are able to make us "wise for salvation through faith in Christ Jesus" (2 Tim 3:15). First Corinthians 1:30 also says that God is the source of our life "in Christ Jesus, who became to us wisdom from God, righteousness and sanctification and redemption." The book of Proverbs teaches us that we really ought to value wisdom and seek it. Both Proverbs and the balance of Scripture teach us that in order to acquire wisdom a relationship with God through Christ is necessary. So biblical wisdom has a thousand practical implications, but it begins with one spiritual reality—a relationship with God through Christ. Once God accomplishes his saving work in our lives on the basis of our faith, we live in a way that is different, holy. The wisdom in the book of Proverbs shows us how to live that way.[4]

WHAT DO THE PROVERBS ACCOMPLISH FOR US?

The book of Proverbs is unique. No other book in the Bible is like it. Why was this book written, compiled, and included as one of the books in the Bible? What is its ultimate purpose? The book itself, in its introduction, clearly states that the writer's goal is "to know wisdom and instruction" (1:2). We see the offer of wisdom stated numerous times in the book. For example, in chapters 1 and 9 a personified Wisdom is poetically portrayed as shouting in the streets, raising her voice over the din of the marketplace, calling to all who will listen and offering wisdom. "How long, O simple ones, will you love being simple? ... If you turn at my reproof, ... I will make my words known to you" (1:22–23). But are there other purposes beyond just the acquisition of wisdom? Let's take a look.

God knows that all of us need to know how to avoid sin in order to live pure lives, and that's a second purpose of the book of Proverbs. The most prominent theme of the first nine chapters is the importance of avoiding sin. For example, the message that adultery leads to suffering could not be more emphatic. "He who does it destroys himself. He will get wounds and dishonor, and his disgrace will not be wiped away" (6:32–33). The same is true for collusion with those who are involved in violence and theft. "Hold back your foot from their paths, for their feet run to evil. ... They set an ambush for their own lives. Such are the ways of everyone who is greedy for unjust gain" (1:15–19). Proverbs also contains warnings against slothfulness, drunkenness, gluttony, lying, and similar sins. Walking in wisdom is walking in righteousness; the way of sin is the way of foolishness.

Knowing that humanity doesn't always take advice to heart, God also needed to convince us of the value of wisdom, and that purpose is prominent in Proverbs. "Blessed is the one who finds wisdom ... for the gain from her is better than gain from silver and her profit better than gold" (3:13–14). Wisdom brings prosperity and long life. Wisdom enables one to live successfully in the world. Such claims underscore the point that wisdom is a precious commodity.

Since it's not enough to know what *not* to do to be holy, God also provides practical instruction in Proverbs to train us how to live daily life. Taken cumulatively, this instruction specifically defines the shape of a godly, successful life. The wise person knows how to relate to family members, has strong relationships, uses words well but does not talk too much, is a hard worker, controls his anger, is sexually moral, is both frugal and generous, and so on.

A final purpose is the real crux of the matter in the book of Proverbs: connecting wisdom to a proper relationship with the one true God. Proverbs 1:7 says, "The fear of the LORD is the beginning of knowledge," and 9:10 states, "The fear of the LORD is the beginning of wisdom." This statement is the repeated spiritual core of the book of Proverbs (1:7; 3:5–6; 9:10; 15:33; see also Job 28:28 and Ps 111:10). Proverbs 1:7 and verses like it supply the indispensable spiritual context of the practical guidance for everyday life. Other cultures had wisdom sayings. However, without proper relatedness to the one true God, practical advice will fall short. In order to live a meaningful life, we must live in accord with the way things really are, and our understanding of the structure of reality is wrong from the outset if it does not include submission to the One who created and sustains everything. The fear of the Lord is an essential part of a relationship with God because he is God and not human. The Bible lists fearing God along with following him, keeping his commandments, listening to his voice, and clinging to him (Deut 13:4). The fear of the Lord is one of the most important concepts in both the Old and New Testaments. In fact, God's people are commanded to fear him (Lev 19:14, 32; 25:17, 36, 43; Eccl 12:13; 1 Pet 2:17). If we seek practical advice in Proverbs and skip the fear of the Lord, we have missed everything.

LISTENING FOR GOD'S WISDOM

The book of Proverbs emphasizes that listening to God in his word is indispensable if we want to access his wisdom and live well. Proverbs 1:20 says, "Wisdom cries aloud in the street, in the markets she raises her voice." Wisdom calls and offers insight to every person. Some people think that wisdom is hard to find. Actually, Wisdom is looking for us, calling to us, and offering us the lessons of living well.

Listening is different than hearing. Hearing is a physical phenomenon. It occurs when sound waves hit our eardrums. Listening is different. We can *hear* God's truth while not *listening*. The Hebrew term translated "listen" can also be translated "to heed." Virtually every parent has given a loud lecture to a child who has a blank look on his face, leading to the parent concluding the lecture by shouting, "DO YOU HEAR ME?!" Of course the child heard—and so did the neighbors. But the intent of the question was not to determine whether the sound waves reached the child's ears. The parent actually meant something like, "Are you receiving this exhortation favorably?" But that doesn't sound as emphatic. Similarly, Wisdom asks us, "I am calling to you! Are you listening?"

Listening to God's Wisdom is complicated by the fact that God's voice has competition. Proverbs 1:21 says, "At the head of the noisy streets she cries out." God's Wisdom shouts over the din, imploring people to listen. Is anything competing with

God's voice today? Sure, hundreds of voices are calling for our attention—the radio, the television, innumerable websites, whatever is playing on our phone. We're always listening to something. God's voice of wisdom has plenty of competition.

When Wisdom calls, we have a choice. Proverbs 1:23 says that Wisdom invites us, "If you turn at my reproof, behold, I will pour out my spirit to you; I will make my words known to you." God calls to us, offering the truth of his word, his wisdom for living. We can ignore him or we can turn to him and listen. When we don't listen, the consequences are disastrous. In Proverbs 1:24 Wisdom says, "I have called and you refused to listen," and the following verses describe what happens when wisdom is refused. Verses 26 and 27 mention "calamity," "terror," "distress and anguish." Those are the consequences of refusing wisdom.

A young man came to me for help in putting his wrecked life back together. He had corresponded with a teenage girl online. They foolishly discussed sensual topics, and when he found out she lived in the same state he visited her for a liaison. A neighbor saw him enter her home through a side door while her parents were not home. The neighbor called the police, the young man was arrested and charged with taking indecent liberties with a minor, and when I talked with him he was facing a criminal trial. That young man had been involved in a Bible-teaching church. Many times he had heard God offering his wisdom. But when he faced the choice of turning to God's wisdom or away from it, he refused wisdom. Wisdom was right in front of him, but he walked away from it. As a result, he was in my office crying with his head in his hands, facing years of consequences.

When people experience the consequences of rejecting wisdom, instead of *wisdom* calling, the tables will be turned, and *they* will call to wisdom. Wisdom says, "Then they will call upon me," but at that point it will be too late: "I will not answer; they will seek me diligently but will not find me" (1:28). They rejected wisdom, they suffered for it, and then suddenly they wanted some wisdom. That's not the way it works. We can't take a dose of wisdom like a magic pill that makes problems instantly disappear. We can't neglect wisdom, get in a jam because of our foolish decisions, and then instantly get wisdom to get us out of the jam. It takes time to learn God's wisdom. When we face a challenge, temptation, or decision, if we respond wisely it will be because long before that moment we turned to God's wisdom, sat at his feet, and let him teach us his way.

The alternative to listening to God's wisdom is satisfaction with self. Proverbs 1:32 says, "The simple are killed by their turning away, and the complacency of fools destroys them." The word translated "complacency" means to be at ease. The word is used in the Old Testament to refer to sinful idleness, or a carefree attitude toward the things of God. Ezekiel 16:49 refers to Sodom before its destruction as having an abundance of "prosperous ease." The people of Sodom were being spiritually carefree, and it led to God's judgment. William McKane wrote that this word refers to "the vast and imperturbable self-satisfaction of the man who has nothing to learn from anyone and who is impervious to instruction."[5] That's what it's like to refuse to listen to God's wisdom. We become satisfied with ourselves—no sense of need for God or for his wisdom. But remember, the "complacency of fools destroys them."

Wisdom shouting in the streets is a figurative, symbolic expression. But let's get literal. How do we listen to God's wisdom? First, finish this book! More importantly, allow this book to introduce you to the power of God's wisdom, and to all of God's word in the Bible. God has given us his word as a revelation of who he is, what he expects of us, and how to live a life that's happy, healthy, and holy. So, read God's word, listen to it, get in a Bible study group, listen to the preaching and teaching of God's word.

A second way we listen to God's wisdom is in prayer. Most of us think of prayer as *talking* to God. It is, but we also need to learn to *listen* to God in prayer. The Holy Spirit lives in every follower of Jesus. The Holy Spirit is able to speak to us. Have you been listening? A caveat: we must not place the spiritual intuitions we receive in prayer on the same level as Scripture, so when we believe God is communicating something to us we must make sure it agrees with Scripture. Still, God's wisdom is available. Listen.

James 1:5–11 exhorts us to pray for wisdom. Verse 5 says, "If any of you lacks wisdom, let him ask of God, who gives generously to all without reproach, and it will be given him." That's a simple plan for anyone who wants wisdom—"let him ask of God." James 1:5 also contains a promise: "It will be given him." God doesn't say, "I'll give wisdom to some people, but not to you." No, God says that when we ask him for wisdom, he gives it. Or as Wisdom says in Proverbs 8:17, "Those who seek me diligently find me."

James 1:6 adds a prerequisite to our prayer for wisdom. We must "ask in faith, with no doubting." James explains what he means in James 1:6 and 8. Verse 6 describes the one who has no faith as unstable, "like a wave of the sea that is driven and tossed by the wind." When we look at the waves on the beach, we can't predict how many waves will rise or how high they will rise. It's random. That's the way it is with someone who doesn't have faith—he's back and forth; one never knows exactly where he stands; he's unstable. James used the word "unstable" in verse 8, and in the same verse he described the doubter as "double-minded"—*dipsychos*, having "two psyches," or "two souls." Will a double-minded person develop God's wisdom? No, because he can't make up his mind whether he's going to listen to God's wisdom or Dr. Phil's. One day he reads the Bible as his source of wisdom, and the next day he checks his horoscope and reads a book on positive thinking. God is not withholding wisdom from him; rather, the man can't decide to receive it. But once we desire wisdom and ask God for it in faith, God promises that he will give it.

A third way we listen to God's wisdom is by paying attention to the way God's wisdom is confirmed in the lives of people around us. We have heard many times, "We learn from our mistakes." Personally, I would prefer to learn from the mistakes of others. If I learn only from my mistakes, I'll have to make a lot of mistakes to become wise. I'd rather not. When someone lives contrary to God's wisdom and they suffer for it, we should learn the lesson: don't live that way because suffering is the result. Proverbs 19:25 says, "Strike a scoffer, and the simple will learn prudence." The simple person is someone who has not yet become wise. Sometimes the word is translated "naive." The simple person learns from seeing a scoffer suffer the consequences of his wrongdoing.

Imagine if a mother told her little son's schoolteacher, "My son is naive. To keep him from acting badly, make sure you punish all the other children for their misbehavior, and he'll learn." That would be a weird request, but it's the idea of Proverbs 19:25: "Strike a scoffer, and the simple will learn prudence." Similarly, Proverbs 21:11 says, "When a scoffer is punished, the simple becomes wise." Yes, we learn God's wisdom by observing the painful consequences of not having it. We also learn wisdom by accepting wisdom's invitation to listen. Hawkers at the county fair call out to us, "Step right up! A winner every time!" When we accept their invitation, we usually don't win. But when we accept wisdom's invitation and listen, we always win. God's wisdom for living well is available.

COMMUNICATING TRUTH WITH WIT

A genre is a form of communication. In fact, everything is communicated by means of some genre. Advertisements, historical narratives, blogs, news articles, and emails are all examples of forms of communication—genres. God's communication with humanity, the Bible, is also in the form of various genres, like narrative, law, poetry, proverbs, prophecy, letters, and apocalyptic.

The book of Proverbs has two sections, and they are different genres. The first nine chapters are usually referred to as instruction literature. The instruction literature is primarily in the form of exhortations from a parent or wisdom teacher to young people in order to motivate them to seek wisdom. Derek Kidner has called these "miniature essays."[6] Proverbs 10–31 is in the genre of sentence literature. The sentence literature is composed of proverbs—two-line sayings, aphorisms that cleverly communicate some truth about life.

Proverbs usually express a truism about life in a succinct way. Ted Hildebrandt has defined a biblical proverb as "a short, salty, concrete, fixed, paradigmatic, poetically-crafted saying."[7] John Russell's epigram is that a proverb contains "the wisdom of many and the wit of one." In other words, many people are aware of the truth communicated by the proverb, but only one person expressed the truth in a concise, catchy way so it could be eloquently communicated and easily remembered. As Cervantes, the 16th century novelist, put it, "Proverbs are short sentences, drawn from long experience."[8]

Witty statements like proverbs powerfully communicate truth. One of my favorites is Proverbs 11:22: "Like a gold ring in a pig's snout is a beautiful woman without discretion." What a vivid and evocative picture: "That ring of gold certainly is beautiful. I would love to approach it, but I don't think I'm going to be able to get over the fact that it's stuck in the filthy nose of that pig." The proverb teaches by making a comparison; it explains something that may be unclear to students by referring to something else that is perfectly clear.

PRINCIPLES, NOT PROMISES

Proverbs are not absolute promises, and we should not interpret them as if they are. Proverbs present the typical consequences of correct or incorrect behavior. For example, a modern proverb is "Smile, and the world will smile back at you." That's generally true. Most of the time, people are more likely to be friendly to us if we are friendly to them. But it's not an absolute promise. Sometimes we encounter people who are determined to be dour no matter how much we smile at them. Similarly, most of the biblical proverbs express general principles of life that prove true in most cases. Missing this fact about the nature of proverbs can lead to mistakes in interpretation.

For example, Proverbs 10:3 says, "The LORD does not let the righteous go hungry, but he thwarts the craving of the wicked." That is generally true, especially in light of eternal rewards. God blesses righteousness. However, many righteous people have suffered and even starved. Proverbs 10:3 is not an absolute promise; it is a proverb that expresses the way life generally works.

AN AUTHOR WHO KNEW WISDOM

The book of Proverbs contains five notations about authorship. The first three name Solomon as the author of those sections (1:1; 10:1; 25:1). Proverbs 30:1 and 31:1 attribute those chapters to two unknown men, Agur and Lemuel. Solomon, the son of King David, was the third king of Israel. The book of 1 Kings states that Solomon was wise because he asked

God for "an understanding mind," and God gave it to him (1 Kgs 3:5–15). So, why does the book of Proverbs have such power to change our lives? The author of most of Proverbs was an extraordinarily wise man, and the source of his wisdom was God himself!

First Kings extols the wisdom of Solomon and states that he "spoke 3,000 proverbs, and his songs were 1,005" (4:32–33). He also had significant contact with Egypt (1 Kgs 9:16, 24; 10:28–29), so he was likely aware of Egyptian wisdom literature. In light of this ancient information about Solomon, it is not surprising that he produced the wise proverbs attributed to him in this book of the Bible. Unfortunately, the record shows that Solomon later strayed from God and lived foolishly. He descended into a sinful lifestyle and worshiped other gods (1 Kgs 11:1–11). Solomon blew it. He had experienced the power of God's wisdom, but then he threw it away. Solomon's life serves as a solemn warning to us—God's wisdom does not come with a lifetime guarantee. To live wisely and well requires that every day we fear God, listen to his wisdom, and lean on him for help to apply that wisdom. Every day.

The repeated use of "my son" as a form of address in Proverbs seems to indicate that the original setting of instruction was the family. Probably much of the book of Proverbs was originally Solomon's instruction of his own son(s) in preparation for leadership in the kingdom. Then, after Solomon wrote the proverbs, they continued to be used in families and in more formal educational settings to train scribes, sages, and future leaders.

So, ever since Solomon's lifetime, the book of Proverbs has been showing people the path to living well. As we begin our journey on that path, even before we take the first steps, maybe it would be helpful to pause for a moment and consider the significance of what we are about to do. We will encounter divine wisdom that has the potential to change our lives for the better. Are we ready to trust God and actively listen to him so we can receive the full benefit of his wisdom? As your guide on this journey, I hope we're prepared. The potential rewards are virtually limitless.

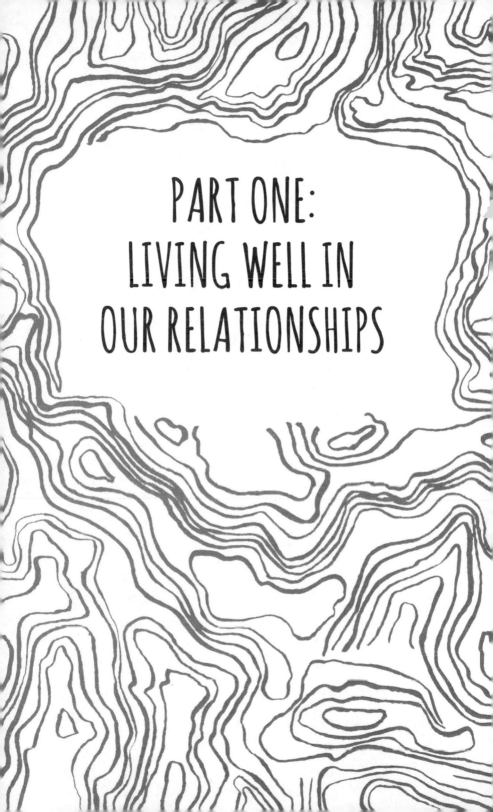

PART ONE: LIVING WELL IN OUR RELATIONSHIPS

CHAPTER 1

PEOPLE SKILLS

In a scene in the movie *Napoleon Dynamite*, Napoleon and his friend Pedro are talking about relating to girls. The goal is to get a date to a high school dance. "Girls like guys with skills," Napoleon says, "Like nun-chucks skills, computer hacking skills." Napoleon thought those were cool skills, but they proved to be irrelevant in helping him find a date. Still, Napoleon had one thing right: girls like guys with skills— people skills!

People skills are essential to success in every area of life. A businessman called me one night to ask me to help one of his employees. He didn't *have to* be concerned for this man's personal life. Helping him had no direct financial benefit for the employer's business, but he cared about this man, and he wanted to help him. I've known this businessman for years. He's been very successful, and one of the keys to his success has been his skill in building quality interpersonal relationships and investing in people.

Sometimes I receive calls from members of church committees that are considering hiring a man I know as their minister. They almost always ask about the man's people skills. "Does he relate to people well? Do people like him?" As our sons were growing up, I tried to teach them that gaining information through formal education is important. However, I also told them that no matter what they may do in adult life, to do it well they would need more than information. They would also need to know how to relate to people well.

In 2011 David Brooks published a book entitled *The Social Animal* that reached the top of the *New York Times* Best Seller list. Brooks cites a mountain of research that indicates that our relationships with people affect everything about us, including the level of success we may achieve. This starts early, with the kinds of attachments we develop with family members, and it continues throughout adulthood with the quality of relationships we build with peers, friends, and coworkers. Brooks' thesis is that our subconscious minds powerfully affect our success, and our subconscious minds are innately social.

The research reflected in Brooks' book corroborates what God's word tells us about how God made us. After God made the first man, he said, "It is not good that the man should be alone" (Gen 2:18). So, God made a companion for the man. God's design for us is to be with other people, not alone. God said that it's "not good" to be alone. So, Adam and Eve were together, and they started a family. Their son Cain killed his brother Abel. God judged him by sending him away from other people; God made him "a fugitive and a wanderer on the earth" (Gen 4:12). Later, when people in the city of Babel rebelled against God, God again judged them by separating them from one another. That's the pattern God established from the beginning—being alone is not good; being in relationships with other people is good. God blesses us by putting us with other people, and he judges us by separating us from other people. That creation pattern is played out throughout the biblical narrative all the way to the descriptions of the New Testament church as a body with interrelated parts. So, when scientists write that humans are hardwired for relationships and that our subconscious minds are innately social, they're writing what the Bible says about us. In order for us to become all God intends for us to be, we need one another.

Yes, we need people skills, but just because we *want* relationships and *need* relationships doesn't necessarily mean that we'll be any good at relationships. All kinds of relationships fail all the time—marriages, friendships, relationships with coworkers and fellow students, and even relationships in the church.

In the book of Proverbs, God has given us wisdom concerning relationships. If we learn that wisdom and live it, we'll have people skills. As we learned earlier, much of the book of Proverbs was written by Solomon. First Kings 3:12 says that God gave Solomon "a wise and discerning mind." Immediately after God blessed Solomon with wisdom, Solomon began to demonstrate that wisdom through people skills. Two women came to him bringing one baby, and each woman claimed that the baby was hers. The situation seemed unsolvable; it was one person's word against another's. But Solomon listened to them, understood the situation, and proposed a solution that succeeded in identifying the real mother. People were amazed that Solomon was able to untangle that relationship dilemma (1 Kgs 3:16-28). Solomon also established an elaborate system of administrative leaders who organized the kingdom (1 Kgs 4:1-25). He built international relationships that resulted in an extensive trade enterprise (1 Kgs 10:14-29). Unfortunately, later Solomon abandoned God's wisdom and resorted to worldly wisdom when he married multiple women to strengthen his international alliances (1 Kgs 9:16; 11:1–9). But Solomon built a strong kingdom on his wisdom in relationships, and the book of Proverbs contains his God-inspired wisdom.

Parents and teachers in ancient Israel used these proverbs to train young people for leadership positions in business and government.[1] Solomon was a successful leader, and if young people wanted to be successful they would learn the principles of God's wisdom that Solomon recorded. Since God inspired these principles and since they are therefore perfect and eternal, we too can use them to help us relate to other people wisely. If we want to live well, we need quality relationships! In this chapter we'll look at five principles in the book of Proverbs concerning all our relationships, and then we'll narrow our focus and look specifically at friendships.

BE CAREFUL ABOUT SELECTION

Selecting persons with whom we will have a relationship sounds elitist, but it's not. Proverbs 13:20 says, "Whoever walks with the wise becomes wise, but the companion of fools will suffer harm." Proverbs 22:24–25 says, "Make no friendship with a man given to anger, nor go with a wrathful man, lest you learn his ways and entangle yourself in a snare." That's not elitist or judgmental; it's wise. Selection of our companions or friends should have nothing to do with their social standing, economic status, or ethnicity. It should have to do with their morality and the inevitable influence they will have on us and the influence we can have on them. If we want to be wise, we will maintain a balance between the influence that flows *to* us and the influence that flows *from* us. On the one hand, we will want influence to flow *to* us from wise people. On the other hand, we also want influence to flow *from* us to people who are not walking in wisdom. We will want to help them because we love them. Jesus is a perfect example here. He spent time with sinners and he influenced them toward God and good. In a similar way, if we want to be wise we will spend time with people who don't know God so we can influence them to know him and his wisdom. And we will spend large amounts of time with wise people so we can learn their wisdom.

When I was in college, I heard someone say that this time next year you will be the same as you are now except for the people you spend time with and the books you read. That statement is largely correct. The people with whom we share our lives shape us. In fact, they can make us or break us. Someone has said that it's hard to soar with eagles if you spend your time with turkeys. The book of Proverbs says that it's hard to live wisely if you spend your time with people who are living foolishly. Our companions affect us.

Did you notice the warning in the verses we cited earlier? Don't associate with a hot-tempered man, "lest you learn his ways and entangle yourself in a snare," and "the companion of fools will suffer harm." How many people are addicted to alcohol or other drugs today because years ago they were just hanging out with people who did that sort of thing? During an impressionable time, they were with people who were doing it, they tried it, and the result was that they were trapped. In the words of Proverbs, they entangled themselves in a snare, and they have suffered harm. How many people have had to suffer the pain of divorce because they married someone who never had the proper commitment? Their marriage was the consequence of spending a lot of time with that person and becoming emotionally involved. This is why parents ought to be concerned about the companions of their children and teenagers. This is why young people ought to listen to the counsel of godly parents about their friends. When parents tell their children that they're spending too much time with the wrong crowd, young people sometimes wonder, "What's the big deal?" But their parents have seen the pain people experience because of being around the wrong people, and they're trying to protect their children from suffering harm. "The companion of fools will suffer harm."

The book of Proverbs not only warns about the negative impact relationships can have on us; it also affirms their positive impact. The first line in Proverbs 13:20 is, "Whoever walks with the wise becomes wise." If we want to control our anger, we should spend time with people who control their anger. If we want to learn humility, we need to hang out with people who aren't full of themselves and who serve other people. If we want to be more faithful in prayer, we need to spend time with people who pray a lot. If we want to be less materialistic, we should hang out with generous givers. You get the picture: "Whoever walks with the wise becomes wise." So, selecting our companions is not elitist or judgmental, and it doesn't mean that we don't relate to people who aren't living wisely. We do *relate* to them in order to influence them for good and for God's glory. But we don't make them our *close* companions, lest they influence *us*. God knows that living well includes following his wisdom about relationships. Be careful about selection.

AVOID DISSENSION

Proverbs 20:3 says, "It is an honor for a man to keep aloof from strife, but every fool will be quarreling." Arguing takes no wisdom. Some people actually boast about telling someone off, but should that really be a source of pride? Even children can argue. One sign of wisdom is the ability to *avoid* dissension. Children like to walk *through* mud puddles; adults walk *around* them. "It is an honor for a man to keep aloof from strife."

Proverbs 17:14 says, "The beginning of strife is like letting out water, so quit before the quarrel breaks out." What a vivid picture! The New International Version (NIV) has, "Starting a quarrel is like breaching a dam." Do you remember the breaking of the levies in New Orleans after Hurricane Katrina? It started with just a weakening of one spot in one dam, then a crack in the dam, and once the water began to pour through, it wasn't long before the dam was destroyed and the city flooded. The Holman Christian Standard Bible renders this statement in this way: "To start a conflict is to release a flood." Here's the wisdom of this verse: before we do or say anything that may be contentious or may ignite a quarrel, we ought to think about the potential damage that could be done to precious relationships. "To start a conflict is to release a flood."

Proverbs 18:19 makes a similar point, but with a different analogy. It says, "A brother offended is more unyielding than a strong city, and quarreling is like the bars of a castle." "The bars of a castle"—that's another powerful analogy. Quarrels forge steel bars between people; they create barriers. Reconciliation can be as hard as getting through prison bars or conquering a fortified city. In other words, once we create dissension, it's really tough to move beyond it.

A parenthetical point should be added here. Sometimes we *have to* accept dissension as a reality that cannot be avoided. If we have to say that wrong is right and the truth is not true in order to maintain peace, then the price for peace is too high. Sometimes we have to accept dissension as a part of what Paul calls "the good fight" of faith (2 Tim 4:7). We can still be sweet to people who deny the truth, but we can't compromise the truth just because it creates conflict or even persecution. And wisdom is knowing when to fight and when to be a peacemaker. The Bible says that the Christian life *is* a fight against sin, Satan, and the self-life. But we should remember that Ephesians 6:12 says, "We do not wrestle against flesh and blood"; Jesus said, "Blessed are the peacemakers" (Matt 5:9); and Romans 12:18 says, "If possible, so far as it depends on you,

live peaceably with all." If we want to be wise about relationships, we'll avoid dissension.

CONTROL EMOTIONS

An entire chapter in this book is devoted to anger because of
its prominence in the book of Proverbs, but we should mention anger here because it can have such profoundly negative
effects on relationships. Proverbs 15:18 says, "A hot-tempered
man stirs up strife, but he who is slow to anger quiets contention." In the Old Testament, just as today, heat or becoming
hot is associated with anger (Gen 30:2; Deut 32:22; "he was hot
under the collar"), but we can be hot with other emotions too.

It's rarely the *subject* of a disagreement that leads to contention between people. It's usually the way we *handle* the disagreement. When hot emotion is added, it obstructs expres-
sions of love, and the result is conflict. Husbands and wives
can get in heated arguments that go on for hours, or even days,
and after a while they can't even remember what started the
original disagreement. It wasn't the issue that created the conflict; it was the hot response to the issue. Somebody, or maybe
everybody, became emotional—they were angry or hurt—
and instead of allowing God's wisdom and Spirit to govern
their responses, their emotions governed their responses.

Someone who's hot with emotion can harm relationships,
even with people they love. But the opposite is also true. Proverbs 16:7 says, "When a man's ways please the LORD, he makes
even his enemies to be at peace with him."

In November of 2005, Dr. Russ Bush was diagnosed with
cancer. A little over two years later, he died at only sixty-three
years old. Dr. Bush taught Christian philosophy his entire adult
life. He was a wonderful husband and father, he wrote several
important books, and he was the academic vice president at
the school where I teach. He and I worked closely together for

about ten years in the administration of the school, and we were good friends. He first came to our school in 1988, during tumultuous days. Russ was hired by the president to help move the school in a more conservative direction. Because he was theologically conservative, the faculty expressed their opposition against hiring him by voting unanimously against the decision. Amazingly, he took the job anyway. After he arrived, faculty members continued to work against him. Russ and his wife, Cindy, felt the sting, but they never responded in kind. They always found ways to express kindness to those who disagreed with them. When a family member of a professor was sick, Russ and Cindy visited and took a meal or a gift. Russ took time to get to know faculty members' children. Though Russ had to disagree with the more liberal faculty, he always did so in a kind way. Years later, at Russ's funeral, I was surprised to see a member of that original faculty who opposed him. I knew him, so I sidled up to him and said that I was really glad he was there. He said, "Russ and I were really good friends." You could have knocked me over with a feather. I had no idea that Russ had managed to become friends with this man who had opposed him. Immediately, I thought of that verse—"When a man's ways please the LORD, he makes even his enemies to be at peace with him." Russ left quite an example for us. When someone opposes us, even though we may feel hurt or anger, we don't have to respond with heat. We can respond in love, but to do that we'll have to control emotion.

LEARN COMMUNICATION

Relationships are all about communication. People who are good at relationships are good at communicating. God's people ought to be experts at communicating with people. The book of Proverbs has a lot to say about how to speak to people, and if we're serious about living wisely, we'll learn and live what it says. If we *don't* communicate well, it's very difficult to build quality relationships. In fact, Proverbs 11:9 says, "With his mouth the godless man would destroy his neighbor." "Destroy"—poor or sinful communication with our neighbors can cause a lot of damage in their lives.

Consider three principles of communication that relate directly to wisdom in relationships. The first is the principle of *sensitivity*. If we're going to be wise in relationships, when we speak we'll be sensitive to the feelings of other people. Proverbs 27:14 says, "Whoever blesses his neighbor with a loud voice, rising early in the morning, will be counted as cursing." *That* is a hilarious proverb! If you want to have a good relationship with your next-door neighbor, don't run your lawn mower at seven o'clock on Saturday morning. Don't bless your friend with a loud voice early in the morning: "Good morning! The wife and I were just out for an early morning walk, and we didn't want to be rude and walk by without speaking!" It will be reckoned a curse to you.

The point is to be sensitive about the right time to talk. For example, it's completely acceptable for husbands and wives to say something like, "I know what you're talking about is important, but this is just not a good time for me. I'm too tired and too emotional about this." Then they simply schedule another time to talk about it. The point of Proverbs 27:14 is that even when we're *blessing* someone, if we do it in the wrong way or at the wrong time, it won't help the relationship. If we want to build relationships with expert communication, we'll be sensitive to the feelings of other people.

A second principle of communication is the principle of *self-control*. Proverbs 15:1 says, "A soft answer turns away wrath, but a harsh word stirs up anger." That works in real life. I've been spoken to in anger—shouted at in anger—and I've seen how answering in a soft and loving way dissolves anger.

In fact, here's a great statement of commitment you could consider making right now: "No matter how angry someone may be at me, I refuse to respond in anger, and I resolve to give a soft answer every time." It's the principle of self-control. Remember, however, that Galatians 5:23 says that self-control is a fruit of the Holy Spirit. The strength to control ourselves comes from God's Spirit, so, when we're tempted to speak in anger, we turn to God and ask him to help us. We control ourselves with the spiritual power he gives us. That's a major principle of godly communication: "A soft answer turns away wrath, but a harsh word stirs up anger."

A third principle of wise communication is the principle of *silence*. It's strange that silence is a principle of communication, but when we have God's wisdom we know that sometimes it's best not to say anything. Proverbs 16:28 describes what happens when someone *should* be silent, but he is not. It says, "A dishonest man spreads strife, and a whisperer separates close friends." When someone speaks untrue, slanderous words, strife spreads and dissension is created. Such words should never be spoken.

Proverbs 17:9 says, "Whoever covers an offense seeks love, but he who repeats a matter separates close friends." Suppose someone wrongs you. What are you going to do about it? You could report to mutual acquaintances how badly you were treated. That might make you feel better, and it would serve that person right for everybody to know what he did. You could even make it sound spiritual and say, "We need to pray for this person who acted so horribly toward me." Proverbs 17:9 describes the outcome of that kind of talk: "He who repeats a matter separates close friends." Next time we're wronged, why don't we ask, "What would be the loving way for me to respond?" If we ask that question sincerely, Proverbs 17:9 provides an answer: "Whoever covers an offense seeks love." What do we do when we seek love? We don't blab to everyone about how badly someone behaved.

EXPRESS AFFECTION

Proverbs 17:17 says, "A friend loves at all times." If we want quality relationships, we have to find ways to express love to people. We just saw that Proverbs 17:9 says, "Whoever covers an offense seeks love." In our relationships, we have to stop thinking about what would make us feel better and start thinking about how we can serve the other person.

Jesus said that the second greatest commandment is, "You shall love your neighbor as yourself" (Mark 12:31). That's a command from God. We cannot be wise about relationships unless we obey what God says, and he tells us to love other people. And don't be confused by distorted ideas about love. Loving people does not mean that we have a warm, gushy feeling every time we think of them. It means serving them, giving to them, and making them more important than ourselves.

The self-life is so powerful that some people have looked at Jesus' command and still focused on loving themselves instead of loving others. They say, "Jesus said, 'Love your neighbor as yourself,' so before I love others I have to make sure I love myself. Do I really love myself adequately? Do I think well enough of myself?" Of course they love themselves; just look at the energy they're expending thinking about themselves! Jesus tells us to think about others and love them. Loving them does not mean that we allow them to take advantage of us or even abuse us in the name of "love." Also, loving people does not mean that we affirm everything they want to do. First Corinthians 13:6 says that love "does not rejoice at wrongdoing." Jesus' command has to do with channeling the energy we expend on ourselves to others.

We don't deserve an award for loving ourselves because loving ourselves comes naturally to most of us. Have you ever been on a sports team, and at the end of the season the coach gave out awards for various special accomplishments? A lot of team members don't win an award for special achievement, so sometimes everybody on the team is given a "participation award." We all know that's not much of an award: "You participated. You were on the field and had a pulse. You remained alive until the end of the season, and we wish to honor you for that." That's the award we deserve for loving ourselves. "Congratulations. You loved yourself. You're a human being and you're self-interested. No special achievement here—you get the participation award." No, the people who accomplish something special are those who notice all they do for themselves and start doing that for other people, even when those other people don't deserve it.

That's how Jesus loves us. Romans 5:8 says, "God shows his love for us in that while we were still sinners, Christ died for us." When we were *sinners*, when we deserved his love the least, he loved us so much that he was willing to die as the sacrifice for our sin. We were under God's righteous condemnation, but Jesus' death appeased the wrath of God on our behalf, and in doing that he not only demonstrated what real love is, but when we put our faith in him he took away our sin and made us new so that we are capable of loving others as we ought.

This is the final wisdom on relationships—love people like Jesus loves them and in the power Jesus gives us. In the strength of the flesh, we'll fail to select godly companions, we'll fail at avoiding dissension, and we'll fail at controlling our emotions. But with the power of Jesus in us, we can be like him, "who became to us wisdom from God" (1 Cor 1:30).

FOUR FRIENDSHIP PRINCIPLES

Let's go a step further and look at what God's book of wisdom says to us about deeper, better friendships. Friendships have the potential to affect our lives profoundly and to give us great joy. I hope friendship is a happy subject for you. A lot of people say that they don't have any real friends, so they feel lonely. I think all of us want to experience the happiness of having close friends. The book of Proverbs helps us with that.

THE WISDOM OF LIMITATION

"Limitation" sounds like a weird word to use with respect to friendships. Why would anybody want to limit the number of the number of friends they have? It may surprise some people to hear that the Bible warns against having too many friends. Proverbs 18:24 says, "A man of many companions may come to ruin." Why would it be unwise to have many friends? It's certainly not unwise to have many positive relationships. But it is unwise to have many *friends*, for at least two reasons. First of all, friends are costly. A real friend is someone in whom we invest our time, prayer, and energy. Good friends take a lot of our time. Are they worth it? Absolutely! But, practically speaking, we don't have enough time or emotional capital to develop close friendships with a lot of people and still be close to our families, serve God, go to school, and earn a living. It's a practical impossibility. If we had a lot of people requiring all of that from us, we wouldn't be able to do anything else.

None of us has very many good friends because it's impossible it's difficult to sustain multiple close friendships. All our relationships are important, but they're also different from having a close friend. Most of us could count on one hand, maybe two, the number of people with whom we have close relationships—people we can count on, no matter what. But if we have just three or four really good friends, that's wonderful.

Second, we limit our friendships because a lot of people simply don't qualify to be a close friend to someone who is committed to God. Proverbs 29:27 says, "An unjust man is an abomination to the righteous, but one whose way is straight is an abomination to the wicked." The commitments and lifestyle of God's people are so different that they are inevitably separated from those who live according to different principles, or no principles. The Apostle Paul expressed the same truth in a series of rhetorical questions. He asked, "What partnership has righteousness with lawlessness? Or what fellowship has light with darkness? What accord has Christ with Belial? Or what portion does a believer share with an unbeliever?" (2 Cor 6:14-15). Light and darkness, Christ and Belial. Paul chose the most obvious opposites to communicate the idea that believers and unbelievers are completely different from one another. Certainly we can and should be friends with people who don't know God or believe his truth, but we'll never be able to share with them the deepest and most important realities of our lives.

In fact, 2 Corinthians even has the command, "Do not be unequally yoked with unbelievers" (6:14). The book of Proverbs vividly demonstrates why that separation is wise. In Proverbs 1:10-19, the parent or wisdom teacher warns to stay away from certain kinds of people:

My son, if sinners entice you,
do not consent.
If they say, "Come with us ...
let us ambush the innocent without reason ...
we shall find all precious goods ...
throw in your lot among us ..."
my son, do not walk in the way with them ...
for their feet run to evil. ...
These men lie in wait for their own blood;
they set an ambush for their own lives.
Such are the ways of everyone who is greedy for
unjust gain.

Here's the point. Everybody wants friendships. Everybody wants to feel like they're part of a group. The day will come when some person or group offers us an invitation to be part of their group but, we know that they're doing things that are not wise—sinful, stupid things. God's book of wisdom says, "Do not walk in the way with them." They're doing something that's wrong, and they're going to suffer for it, so the price of being their friend is too high. Don't do it. In fact, James 4:4 says, "Friendship with the world is enmity toward God." We cannot be friendly with the ways of the world and right with God at the same time.

The Wisdom of Loyalty

Loyalty is a wonderful blessing in relationships, and it's usually found only in close friendships. Do you have a friend who is loyal to you? Is there someone who knows you're loyal to him or her? Loyalty is not very common. Proverbs 20:6 says, "Many a man proclaims his own steadfast love, but a faithful man who can find?" It's one thing to *proclaim*, "I'm loyal to you." It's another thing to remain loyal when circumstances test that loyalty. The point of Proverbs 20:6 is that many people claim to love, but few people will actually stand by you no matter what happens.

Loyalty is often the difference between acquaintances and real friends. Acquaintances look like friends, but when the fires of adversity come they're burned away by the heat. True friendships, though, are purified and strengthened by fiery trials. Acquaintances will be with us when it's popular or convenient, but real friends will stand by us no matter what comes. "Many a man proclaims his own steadfast love, but a faithful man who can find?"

Proverbs 18:24 says, "There is a friend who sticks closer than a brother." The verb translated "sticks" is the same verb used in Genesis 2:24 to describe a man leaving his father and mother and "holding fast" to his wife. A true friend holds fast to his friend, through good times and bad times. People all around us are struggling, and they need friends to stick with them. A married couple is having marital struggles that almost nobody knows about. They need a friend to stick with them. Children and teenagers are living on an emotional roller coaster, and they wonder if they really matter to anybody. Will somebody stick with them? Adults are trying to figure out what it means to be a good dad or mom, and they're fighting to be free from guilt over past mistakes. Senior adults are walking around with broken hearts over the wrong choices of their grown children or a spouse's early death. Often, they carry those burdens alone. Is somebody going to stick with them? A true friend is loyal. Be the friend who sticks closer than a brother.

THE WISDOM OF LEARNING

Proverbs 27:17 says, "Iron sharpens iron, and one man sharpens another." God intends for our friendships to sharpen us, or cause us to grow. Not everything can sharpen iron. Butter can't do it. Neither can vinyl or tree bark. Not everything can sharpen a human being. But a real friend can do it. Friendships can have a sanctifying influence on us. A friend can smooth out our rough edges because friendship love is as tough as iron.

Proverbs 27:6 says, "Faithful are the wounds of a friend; profuse are the kisses of an enemy." Judas kissed Jesus in the Garden of Gethsemane, but it was not the greeting of real friendship. Some people make a show of being our friends, but it's a form of deceit because they are not really committed to us no matter what. Real friends are just the opposite. They don't flatter us; they tell us the truth even when it hurts, and they do it to help us. They wound us in the same way a surgeon wounds; they hurt us in order to help us. "Faithful are the wounds of a friend." We can learn from our good friends because they'll be honest with us and talk with us about our need to grow.

The Wisdom of Love

Proverbs 17:17 says, "A friend loves at all times, and a brother is born for adversity." We have often heard the saying, "If you want to have a friend, *be* a friend." Proverbs 17:17 tells us how to do that, to love someone at all times. Such love is not just emotional. Our emotions change; no emotion is "at all times." But friends love at all times—when they feel like it and when they don't. And the love described in Proverbs 17:17 is not conditional. We often place unspoken conditions on our love: "I'll love you if you meet my needs," "I'll love you if you behave the way I expect you to behave," or "I'll love you if it doesn't require much sacrifice on my part." That's not true friendship, because "a friend loves at all times."

The greatest news about friendship is that God is our friend. James 2:23 says that Abraham was "a friend of God." Jesus said to his disciples, "You are my friends if you do what I command you. No longer do I call you servants, for the servant does not know what his master is doing; but I have called you friends, for all that I have heard from my Father I have made known to you" (John 15:14–15). If we know and obey Jesus, he calls us his friends. Therefore, the wisdom of Proverbs concerning friends should characterize the way we relate to him. We're to be loyal to him, learn from him, and love him. And we're to exclude relationships that compete with him.

As for God, all the traits of friendship are found in him perfectly. He is "a friend who sticks closer than a brother" (Prov 18:24). He is loyal. He said, "I will never leave you nor forsake you" (Heb 13:5). Is God unselfish? He said of himself, "The Son of Man came not to be served but to serve" (Matt 20:28). God is also the iron that sharpens us. He is the perfect sanctifying influence. I hope you have several good friends, but I hope most of all that you are a friend of Jesus. We can't live well without him.

QUESTIONS FOR REFLECTION

1. Are any relationships in your life hindering you from living according to God's wisdom? If so, can you think of changes you can make in that relationship?

2. How would you assess how you have been doing at avoiding dissension in your relationships? How would people who know you rate how you are doing?

3. What specific actions have you taken lately to express your love for God and other people?

4. Make a list of people you consider to be good friends. Reflect on how you can strengthen your relationship with each one.

CHAPTER 2

OUR POWERFUL WORDS

Mary Ann Bird was born with a cleft palate. Growing up, she knew she was different, and she hated it. When she started school, she had to endure teasing from her classmates. Children would often ask, "What happened to your lip?" She would tell them that she had fallen as a baby and cut herself on a piece of glass. She thought it was more acceptable to have suffered an accident than to have been born different. She later wrote, "By the age of seven I was convinced that no one outside my own family could ever love me. Or even like me." Then she entered second grade, and Mrs. Leonard's class. She described Mrs. Leonard as "round and pretty and fragrant, with chubby arms and shining brown hair and warm, dark eyes that smiled. ... Everyone adored her. But no one came to love her more than I did. And for a special reason."

Every year the school gave hearing tests. During one part of the test, each child went to the door of the classroom, turned sideways, closed one ear with a finger, and the teacher whispered something from her desk, which the children would repeat. Then, the same thing was done for the other ear. Throughout the testing, little Mary Ann wondered what Mrs. Leonard might whisper to her. The teachers usually said things like, "The sky is blue," or "Do you have new shoes?" Then came Mary Ann's turn. She trudged to the door, turned her ear to Mrs. Leonard, plugging up the other with her finger. This is what Mary Ann Bird later wrote of the next few moments: "I waited, and then came the words that God had surely put into her mouth, seven words that changed my life forever. Mrs. Leonard, the pretty, fragrant teacher I adored, said softly, 'I wish you were my little girl.'"[1]

Yes, words can change our lives. Psychologist Michael Rousell wrote a book entitled *Sudden Influence* based on his decades studying what he calls "Spontaneous Influence Events"—"*spontaneous* because of their inadvertent nature, *influence* because of their powerful effect, and *events* because they occur during significant incidents." He writes, "Some inadvertent comment or critical incident can shape a life profoundly, for good or ill, toward hope or despair." For example, he cites the experience of Les Brown, who became an international speaker on motivation and the owner of a multimillion-dollar business. In his early school years, though, Brown's scores on achievement tests were low—so low that he was labeled "educationally mentally handicapped." That label had a profound effect on Brown's performance and self-esteem, until one day when he told a teacher that he could not answer the teacher's question "because I'm educationally mentally handicapped." The teacher responded angrily, "Don't ever say that again. Someone's opinion of you does not have to become your reality." That one statement completely reframed the way Les Brown thought about himself.[2]

Rousell has described a reality that God revealed to Solomon three thousand years ago—that the words we speak have powerful effects that reach far beyond what most of us real-ize. The book of Proverbs contains 915 verses, and 222 of those verses have to do with some aspect of speech. God has given us an enormous amount of instruction about how to use the gift of speech wisely. Proverbs 18:21 says, "Death and life are in the power of the tongue." Our words can bless, and they can curse. They can help, and they can harm. They can fulfill, and they can kill. As Rudyard Kipling says, "Words are ... the most powerful drug used by mankind."[3] Think of the strongest man you have ever known or seen. Your words are stronger than he is. "Death and life are in the power of the tongue."

Matthew 12:33-35 records that Jesus said, "The tree is known by its fruit. You brood of vipers! How can you speak good, when you are evil? For out of the abundance of the heart the mouth speaks. The good person out of his good treasure brings forth good, and the evil person out of his evil treasure brings forth evil." Jesus' point is that *our words expose our character.* Jesus said that we know a tree by its fruit. When we see apples growing on a tree, we don't usually say, "I wonder what kind of tree that is." We know it's an apple tree because of the apples. Jesus said that, in the same way, the words we speak reveal our character. When we hear foolish or profane speech, we don't have to say, "I wonder what kind of person that is." We know the person's character by his words, just like we know the tree by its fruit. Jesus said, "Out of the abundance of the heart the mouth speaks." What comes out of our mouths is an indication of what's in our hearts. When we squeeze a tube of toothpaste, what comes out is not ketchup but toothpaste. What comes out is what is on the inside. When a pure person is squeezed, what comes out is pure; when an impure person is squeezed, out comes impurity. "Out of the abundance of the heart the mouth speaks." Our words expose our character.

Also, *God will judge us by the words we speak.* Matthew 12:36-37 says that Jesus made an amazing statement. He said,

"On the day of judgment people will give account for every careless word they speak, for by your words you will be justified, and by your words you will be condemned." Jesus said that when we stand before God in judgment, we'll give an account for every careless word that we have spoken. Obviously, God takes the words we speak seriously. That fact ought to cause *us* to take them seriously, and to pray, "God, help me to be careful, not careless, about the words I speak, and show me in your word how I can speak wisely to please you."

In this chapter, we'll learn what God's book of wisdom says about using words positively—six wonderful ways we can use our words. After that, we'll see what God says about sins of speech we should avoid.

SIX WONDERFUL WAYS TO USE WORDS

First, we can use our words *to encourage others*. We can learn to speak in a way that gives people confidence they formerly lacked, we can cheer them on when they're down, and we can support them when they're weak. That's encouragement. Proverbs 15:30 is translated literally in the New American Standard Bible (NASB); it reads, "Good news puts fat on the bones." We may think, "Give me as much bad news as possible! I don't need any more fat!" But in the world in which Solomon lived, it was rare to be fat in the sense of obesity. The presence of fat on the bones simply meant that someone was not starving. He or she was prosperous and healthy. Receiving good news has such a positive effect on us that our health is improved when we hear it.

Proverbs 25:25 says, "Like cold water to a thirsty soul, so is good news from a far country." When we speak good words, it's like giving cold water to someone who's parched. When a man speaks encouraging words to his wife, it can make her day. When parents encourage their children, it can alter their perception of themselves. When wives speak words of encouragement to their husbands, it makes them feel like they can conquer the world. Encouraging words bring us joy.

Encouraging words are powerful words. They can give someone the strength they need to cope with difficulties, and they can give them the confidence that they can do what God is calling them to do. When I was a teenager, I believed God was calling me into vocational ministry. I didn't really know what that meant. I knew I could sing, so I was thinking about music ministry. One day the minister of music in my home church told me, "Someone with your leadership ability ought to be a pastor." I remember thinking, "He thinks I'm capable of being a pastor, so maybe God can use me in that way." Over thirty-five years later, I still remember what he said to me. His words of encouragement made a difference in my life. Wouldn't you like to make a difference in someone's life in that way?

When Mary Kay Wagner graduated from Houston's Reagan High School, she wanted to enter college, but she had no money and wasn't able to get a scholarship. So, instead of going to college, she got married, but after the birth of three children her husband asked for a divorce. At that point, she got two jobs to support herself and her children. One of those jobs was in sales. She went to her company's sales convention, and she saw one of the women who worked for the company crowned the "sales queen." Mary Kay set a goal to become the sales queen at the next year's convention. She even mustered up the courage to tell the president of the company about her goal. She writes about what happened when she told the president of the company about her goal: "He took my hand in both of his, looked me square in the eye and after a moment said, 'Somehow I think you will.' Those five words changed my life." A year later, she *was* crowned the sales queen. She went on to become a successful salesperson, and eventually she founded Mary Kay

Cosmetics. Her life was changed because someone spoke words of encouragement to her. Mary Kay recognized that, and she wanted to do the same thing for others. She writes, "You can do it! So often a woman comes to us who desperately needs to hear that. ... We encourage her."[4] "Like cold water to a thirsty soul, so is good news."

Ephesians 4:29 says, "Let no corrupting talk come out of your mouths, but only such as is good for building up, as fits the occasion, that it may give grace to those who hear." We can build up people with our words. We can use words to give grace to people, to meet their need.

Second, we can use our words *to teach wisdom*. When we develop God's wisdom, our words will be wise. I like the way Proverbs 16:23 expresses it: "The heart of the wise makes his speech judicious and adds persuasiveness to his lips." When our hearts are wise, they make our speech wise. The book of Proverbs affirms that fact several times. Proverbs 10:13 says, "On the lips of him who has understanding, wisdom is found." Proverbs 10:31 says, "The mouth of the righteous brings forth wisdom." Proverbs 15:7 says, "The lips of the wise spread knowledge; not so the hearts of fools."

Once we have God's wisdom, we'll speak wisely, and others will learn wisdom from us. Of course, not everyone is interested in learning wisdom. Proverbs 18:2 says, "A fool takes no pleasure in understanding." Some people don't know wisdom, and they don't want to know. It's a little like men and housework. They think that if they don't know how to do something, they won't be expected to do it. One husband was trying to wash his sweatshirt, but he didn't know anything about the washing machine, so he called to his wife and asked what setting to use on the washing machine to wash his sweatshirt. She shouted back, "Well, what does it say on the sweatshirt?" He said, "University of Oklahoma." Not everybody is ready or willing to be taught. But wise people are ready to learn more wisdom, and those who have wisdom know they help others by teaching it.

Third, we can use our words *to rebuke wrong behavior*. Proverbs 28:23 says, "Whoever rebukes a man will afterward find more favor than he who flatters with his tongue." At first glance that seems like the opposite of the truth. Would people rather that we flatter them or rebuke them? Of course people enjoy flattery more than rebuke, but at some point after someone flatters them, it may occur to them that the flattery was shallow and perhaps not even true. A genuine compliment and flattery are different. Flattering words ring hollow. On the other hand, at some point after someone rebukes us, after the initial pain of the rebuke has passed, we may realize two things: First, it's likely that the person rebuked us because they cared about us and wanted to help us. Second, the rebuke will help us to be better people.

Sometimes we are the ones being rebuked, and sometimes we may be the ones offering correction or rebuke. Either way, exhortation can be a good thing, but we have to be careful about the way we exhort. We have to correct people in the right way—a loving way. We have to be the right person to do the correcting. It is rarely appropriate to exhort someone in authority over us. We have to rebuke someone at the right time—a teachable and private time. We have to exhort for the right reason—to help them, not just to get something off our chest. In fact, when we *want* to correct someone, usually we should not do it. We're ready to exhort someone when we hate the idea of doing it, but we know that if we do it we could help the other person.

When I was in high school, my English teacher for two years was Mrs. Catherine Weldon. She was a great English teacher, and she loved literature. At the time, however, I didn't appreciate Mrs. Weldon as much as I should have. One day, she said something to the class, and I remember rolling my eyes in a smart-aleck way because, of course, I already knew everything she was saying. Just as I was rolling my eyes, Mrs. Weldon looked at me and saw what I did. After class, she asked me to stay and talk with her. I'll never forget the lecture she gave me. She didn't put me down, or even criticize me, for my bad attitude, though I certainly deserved it. In fact, she did just the opposite. She told me that she respected me and even saw me as a friend. She said that somebody like me should be an example for the other students. She said that because she looked at me in that way, she was really disappointed that I would act that way toward her and have such a surly, disrespectful attitude. When she finished talking to me in such a sweet way, I felt about one millimeter tall. I was so ashamed. I knew that not only did I deserve her rebuke, I also knew that she had done it in a gracious way and only because she wanted to help me. Proverbs 25:15 says, "A soft tongue will break a bone." Her words to me were so soft, but she broke me with them exactly where I needed to be broken. She helped me with her rebuke.

A fourth way we can use our words positively is *to restore relationships*. Relationships can be wounded deeply by the words we speak, but relationships can also be helped by the way we speak. Proverbs 15:1 says, "A soft answer turns away wrath, but a harsh word stirs up anger." We can stop an argument and cool someone's anger by using gentle words. On the other hand, we can stir up an argument by the way we speak. When someone says something we don't like, we can say, "That's stupid!" or we can say, "Could you help me understand that?" When someone says something that causes our anger to rise, we could say, "You really tick me off!" or we could say, "Would you mind if we talked about this a little later?" By the words we use, we can damage a relationship, or we can contribute to the health of the relationship. One of the most common reasons for divorce is poor communication. The way husbands and wives communicate with one another can make or break their marriage.

When we use the right words, it not only helps the relationship, but we feel better too. Proverbs 15:23 says, "To make an apt answer is a joy to a man, and a word in season, how good it is!" When we speak in a mean way, or we speak in anger to get something off our chest, we may think it will make us feel better to say it. Just the opposite is true. We feel better when we are careful to choose the right word, the most helpful and loving word. "To make an apt answer is a joy to a man, and a word in season, how good it is!"

Proverbs 15:28 says, "The heart of the righteous ponders how to answer." When righteous people ponder how to answer, they have time to ask God, "How should I respond?" Sometimes we should wait until we have more information before we speak. Proverbs 18:13 says, "If one gives an answer before he hears, it is his folly and shame." First, we listen carefully to all the issues, then we speak. Of course, silence *can* be used as a weapon. Spouses give one another "the silent treatment." Or they say, "Well, if you don't know, I'm not going to tell you." The obvious question is, how can they possibly know if you don't tell them? The person who gains God's wisdom knows when to speak and how to speak. "The heart of the righteous ponders how to answer."

A fifth positive use of our words is *to confess sin*. Proverbs 28:13 expresses an important truth: "Whoever conceals his transgressions will not prosper, but he who confesses and forsakes them will obtain mercy." The book of Proverbs gives us wisdom so that we'll prosper in every way. Proverbs 28:13 says that we will *not* prosper if we conceal our transgression. Unconfessed sin is a barrier to living well. Unconfessed sin dirties our souls, dominates our minds, discourages our emotions, and even damages our health. This is what King David wrote about his unconfessed sin:

> Blessed is the man against whom the Lord counts no
>   iniquity,
> and in whose spirit there is no deceit.
> For when I kept silent, my bones wasted away
> through my groaning all day long.
> For day and night your hand was heavy upon me;
> my strength was dried up as by the heat of summer.
> (Ps 32:2–4)

Those are the words of a miserable man. He felt bad in his spirit and in his body. Maybe the most miserable person in the world is not an unredeemed person whose mind is darkened concerning sin, but a redeemed person who has fallen into sin. As pastor and author Adrian Rogers became well-known for saying, "An unsaved man leaps into sin and loves it, but a Christian lapses into sin and loathes it."

The answer for the misery that results from sin is confession. "Whoever conceals his transgressions will not prosper, but he who confesses and forsakes them will obtain mercy." First, we ask God's Spirit to reveal our sin to us, and then we grieve over what has grieved the heart of God. Then, we confess our sin to God. We don't merely say, "God, forgive me for all my sins." Instead, in prayer we tell the Lord exactly what we've done; that's confession. The wonderful truth is that the only one who already knows about our sin and who's qualified to condemn our sin is also the one who's willing and able to forgive our sin and to cleanse us of all unrighteousness.

Don't miss the fact that Proverbs 28:13 says that we are to confess our sin *and* forsake it. It's not enough to confess without forsaking. Some Christians have the mistaken idea that they can attend church, shed some tears over their sin, tell God they're sorry, and return to more sin. No wonder they aren't prospering more! They're confessing their sin but not forsaking it. Instead, pray this: "God, I admit to you what I've done, and I ask you to forgive me. I forsake my sin forever, and I choose to walk with you and in your ways." "Whoever conceals his transgressions will not prosper, but he who confesses and forsakes them will obtain mercy."

A sixth positive use of our words is *to profess faith*. Proverbs 9:10 says, "The fear of the LORD is the beginning of wisdom, and the knowledge of the Holy One is insight." Wisdom begins when we relate properly to God. How do we do that? We turn from sin, put our faith in Jesus as our Savior, and we begin following him as Lord. When we do that, we *profess* faith in him.

Romans 10:9 says, "If you confess with your mouth that Jesus is Lord and believe in your heart that God raised him from the dead, you will be saved." We believe in our hearts, and we confess with our mouths. Why is confession of Jesus an integral part of our salvation? Because it's inevitable that what we possess we will profess. If something is in our hearts, we will talk about it. If we have been reconciled to the one true God through Jesus the Savior, if the almighty God of the universe has come to dwell in our hearts by faith, of course we'll talk about it. We will confess with our mouths the Lord Jesus. There is no wiser use of words than to profess faith in Jesus. If you have never done that, why not do it right now? Receive Jesus as your Savior and profess faith in him. Then, once we know him as Lord, we continue to speak of him.

Before Hurricane Katrina, George lived in the Gentilly area of New Orleans. I can relate to George, since my wife and I lived in the Gentilly area during the first two years of our marriage. After Katrina, George's home was a total loss. He evacuated at the last minute with only his dog, Smokey. He went to Alexandria, Louisiana, and lived first in a Red Cross shelter, then a FEMA trailer, and ultimately a larger trailer. George was estranged from his family, and he didn't feel welcome or at home. After more than two years, George was at the end of his rope and felt like he couldn't take any more. He loaded a gun, took his dog Smokey outside, and tied her to the porch. He didn't want her to see what he was about to do. At that moment, some people from Family of Grace Church were visiting door-to-door in George's trailer park. Brad Webb was one of those people. Brad was assigned to one side of the road, but when he saw George tying Smokey to the porch he crossed the road to talk with him. He spoke to George about a relationship with Jesus, and he invited him to come to their church.

Brad's words to George gave him enough hope to survive a little longer, and he attended church that Sunday night. After the service, he asked Brad to pray for him. He said he wanted Jesus in his life, so that night George prayed and put his faith in Jesus. This is what George said about Brad's visit to his trailer at that providential moment: "These people saved me. I was tying my dog up, then [I was going to] go in my house, and shoot myself in the head. These people saved me—them and then my Lord Jesus Christ. Normally, I wouldn't talk to someone going around talking about religion. These people treated me like a real person. They really talked to me."[5]

That's the power of the right words spoken in the right way at the right time. Brad Webb's words literally saved George's life. There could be no greater use of our words than to tell someone about Jesus and the life he gives. What was it that we read in Proverbs 18:21? "Death and life are in the power of the tongue." We can use our words to bless and give life, or we can use our words to blast; to help, or to harm.

SIX WICKED WAYS
OF USING WORDS

We have seen that the book of Proverbs describes six positive uses of our words. We can encourage others, teach wisdom, rebuke wrong behavior, restore relationships, confess sin, and profess faith in Jesus. Those are wonderful ways we can use words. The Bible also describes some wicked ways of using words. We encounter such words virtually every day, and all of us face the challenge of controlling our words. So, let's look in the book of Proverbs to see six ways of using words that we should avoid. Maybe you'll see that you currently speak in such ways. One significant result of this study would be to correct such patterns of speaking so that you speak in a way that helps others and gives glory to God.

The first sinful way we use words is *flattery*. Flattery is not the same as sincere praise. It's not the same as expressing gratitude or heartfelt encouragement. We should speak encouraging words to one another, and we should express gratitude. The difference between flattery and expressing gratitude or encouragement is the motive of the speaker and the truthfulness of the words. People who flatter usually have an ignoble motive for their words. Proverbs 2:16 says that when we acquire God's wisdom, it will watch over us, "So you will be delivered from the forbidden woman, from the adulteress with her smooth words." Flattery is one of the snares used by an adulterous woman. Using "smooth words," she flatters the man she's trying to trap; Proverbs warns us to watch out for it. If a woman tells a man that he looks a lot like George Clooney even though he's not all that handsome, he should watch out. She's using flattery to control him and the situation. Someone has said that flattery is like perfume; it's nice to have around, but it's not meant to be swallowed.

Flattering words are not actually believed by the one who speaks them. Flattery has a motive—to *use* the words to get what the flatterer wants, whatever that may be. Proverbs 26:28 says, "A flattering mouth works ruin." When you're tempted to flatter, don't, because it leads to ruin, not blessing. Judas used flattery when he betrayed Jesus. He went to Jesus in the Garden of Gethsemane, kissed him, and called him "Rabbi." "Rabbi" was a term of respect, but it was flattery here because Judas wasn't complimenting Jesus. He was trapping him. Slanderers say things behind your back that they won't say to your face, but flatterers say things to your face that they would never say behind your back.

We looked at Proverbs 28:23 earlier in the chapter: "Whoever rebukes a man will afterward find more favor than he who flatters with his tongue." A rebuke hurts, but if it's done in the right way for the right reason, afterward if we take the rebuke to heart we'll probably be better people. Flattery works in the opposite way. It doesn't hurt, it's fun to hear, but it has an aftertaste. Later, we realize that the words were not really true and probably were not believed by the one who spoke them. When we flatter someone, we may think we'll find favor, but we won't.

A second sinful way to use words is *boasting*. Proverbs 25:14 says, "Like clouds and wind without rain is a man who boasts of a gift he does not give." Boasting is a particular way of lying. It's bragging about things we didn't do, or claiming credit when we don't deserve credit. Boasting is also glorying in things that are not worthy of glory, like our possessions, position, or abilities—all of which are gifts from God. Samson boasted about his strength, but God had given it to him, and after he boasted God took it from him. When we boast, we set ourselves up for being cut down to size. The book of Daniel describes how King Nebuchadnezzar said, "Is not this great Babylon, which I have built by my mighty power ... and for the glory of my majesty?" But while he was saying those boasting words, "there fell a voice from heaven, 'O King Nebuchadnezzar ... the kingdom has departed from you, and ... your dwelling shall be with the beasts of the field'" (Dan 4:30-32). Immediately God's word concerning Nebuchadnezzar was fulfilled.

We are not to boast. At least, we are not to boast about ourselves. One wonderful use of our words is to boast in the Lord. First Corinthians 1:31 says, "Let the one who boasts, boast in the Lord." Psalm 34:2 says, "My soul makes its boast in the LORD." God is worthy of all our boasting.

A third sinful way to use our words is *lying*. Proverbs 6:16–19 describes seven things the Lord hates. A lot of people are surprised that God hates anything. God doesn't hate any person, but he hates sin, and this passage specifies seven sins that he hates.

> There are six things that the LORD hates,
> seven that are an abomination to him:
> haughty eyes, a lying tongue,
> and hands that shed innocent blood,
> a heart that devises wicked plans,
> feet that make haste to run to evil,
> a false witness who breathes out lies,
> and one who sows discord among brothers.

Of the seven things the Lord hates, at least two of them have to do with lying—"a lying tongue" and "a false witness who breathes out lies." The Lord hates lying. He sees, more clearly than we ever will, how many people are hurt by lies.

My parents told me and my siblings many times that when we do something wrong we make it worse when we try to lie our way out of it. They were right. "Oh what a tangled web we weave, once we practice to deceive." Still, the greatest motivation for honesty is not that we'll get in more trouble when we lie, but that we are avoiding behavior that the Lord hates.

People lie on their income taxes. They lie to their children because it would be more difficult to deal with them if they told the truth. "If you do that, the boogeyman is going to get you." That's not true. Some parents even lie to someone with their children listening and knowing that Mom or Dad is lying. Someone comes to the front door on a Saturday afternoon. Junior tells Dad that a salesman is at the door and is instructed, "Tell him Daddy's not home." So, Junior goes to the door and says, "Daddy said to tell you he's not home."

It's important to note that the Bible doesn't make distinctions between the colors of lies; there's no such thing as a white lie that's preferable to a black lie. A lie is a lie, and God hates a lying tongue.

The fourth sinful way to use words is *talking too much*. Proverbs 17:27 says, "Whoever restrains his words has knowledge." Proverbs 10:19 says, "When words are many, transgression is not lacking, but whoever restrains his lips is prudent." In other words, if we don't think carefully before we speak, we inevitably will say something that we shouldn't. Some people think that if they don't express their opinion about everything, the world will be a poorer place. We don't want to be that person. Surely all of us have had the experience of saying, "Boy, I wish I hadn't said that! If I had just kept my mouth shut!" It's like the saying goes:

> The wise old owl sat in the oak,
> The more he saw, the less he spoke,
> The less he spoke, the more he heard.
> Why can't we all be like that bird?[6]

I once heard someone say, "If all the people in the world who talk too much could be lined up, head to foot lying on their backs, they ought to be left right there." We ought to listen more and talk less.

When we speak rashly, it's not just annoying to other people; it can also be harmful. Proverbs 12:18 says, "There is one whose rash words are like sword thrusts." The thrusts of a sword are not just annoying; they're deadly. When we speak, we're using a sharp instrument. The sharp instrument of speech can be used like a scalpel to do a lot of good, or it can be used to do harm. When a surgeon performs surgery on us, we don't want him to say afterward, "Well, we got all the cancer. We were actually having a lot of fun using the scalpel, so we cut out several other things while we were in there." Similarly, when we like to talk, it's possible to continue talking until we say something that doesn't need to be said and to then find that someone is hurt. When we speak, we're wielding a sharp sword; we don't want to wield it rashly.

Proverbs 17:28 says, "Even a fool who keeps silent is considered wise; when he closes his lips, he is deemed intelligent." I'm banking my life on that verse. Somebody might think I'm wise if I just keep silent. During my growing up years, my mother used to repeat a saying with a similar message: "Better to remain silent and be thought an idiot than to open your mouth and remove all doubt." It's wise to restrain our words.

A fifth wicked use of words is *speaking in anger*. Proverbs 15:1 was quoted above: "A soft answer turns away wrath, but a harsh word stirs up anger." It's amazing how that works in life. A gentle answer really does turn away wrath. When we don't control our anger, we say things that are mean and hurtful. When we're angry, we are reckless and rash with our words. Years ago, Horatio Palmer wrote a hymn entitled "Angry Words."

> Angry words, O let them never
> From the tongue, unbridled slip.
> With the soul's best impulse ever
> Check them, ere they soil the lips
> Angry words are quickly spoken,
> Bitter thoughts are rashly stirred,
> Brightest links of life are broken,
> By a single angry word.[7]

The fondest links of life can be broken by angry words. A young couple gets married, and they're constantly showing affection for one another. They're constantly lovey-dovey to a degree that is truly annoying to everybody around them. "You're so wonderful!" "No, you are!" They're inseparable, and they're clearly in love. Then one day the man gets angry about something and speaks angry words to his wife. The words slash into her heart like shrapnel and wound her affections. It happens all the time, and it damages marriages all the time.

The same thing happens in other precious relationships—in our families and with our friends. Sure, we can apologize for those words, but we can't take them back any more than we can bring back an arrow we've shot or cause flowing water to reverse its course. Speaking in anger has done so much damage to so many people. I've counseled adults who still remember something their mom or dad said to them when they were young. Decades later it's still hurting them. How much better to ask God to help us handle our anger, and refrain from speaking angry words?

Speaking in anger also causes us to speak rashly, before we hear all the facts. Proverbs 18:13 says, "If one gives an answer before he hears, it is his folly and shame." When I was a young pastor, I talked with a few men who were in the midst of separating from their wives, and as they described their wives I thought, "What a horrible woman she is! This man is a saint for having lived with her this long. We ought to give him a Purple Heart for all he's had to endure." Later I talked with the wives, and after they described their husbands I thought, "What an awful person *he* is! How has this wife refrained from doing bodily harm to him?" I realize that in marriage sometimes it *is* one person's fault, but most of the time we're not able to make a fair appraisal of any situation until we hear both sides. If we speak in anger, reacting to partial facts, we speak foolishly. "If one gives an answer before he hears, it is his folly and shame." We should use gentle words or remain silent.

The sixth wrong way of speaking is *gossip*. Probably everyone reading this has been gossiped about, and probably everyone knows someone we would classify as a gossip, like the person who said, "I never repeat anything unless it's good." Proverbs 26:20 says, "For lack of wood the fire goes out, and where there is no whisperer, quarreling ceases." A small problem can become big if someone talks about it enough. On the other hand, a big problem often becomes small and disappears if we don't stir it up by talking about it. Has anyone ever said to you, "Well, I shouldn't repeat this, but ..." Just tell them, "If you shouldn't repeat it, then please don't."

Consider four qualities of gossip. First of all, gossip is *desirable*. Proverbs 18:8 says, "The words of a whisperer are like delicious morsels; they go down into the inner parts of the body." "Like delicious morsels"—gossip is pleasurable. If it didn't bring some pleasure, why would people do it all the time?

Second, gossip is *divisive*. Proverbs 16:28 says, "A dishonest man spreads strife, and a whisperer separates close friends." When we speak behind someone's back, spreading gossip, the result is separation, even between close friends.

Third, gossip is *disloyal*. Proverbs 20:19 says, "Whoever goes about slandering reveals secrets; therefore do not associate with a simple babbler." Gossip reveals secrets and betrays confidences. When we're loyal to someone, we keep their confidences, but gossip is disloyal.

Fourth, gossip is *destructive*. Proverbs 11:9 says, "With his mouth the godless man would destroy his neighbor." *Destroy*. Before we repeat something we have heard, we should realize that it may not be true. Second, even if it's true, it's likely that it's not necessary to repeat it. Third, if we do repeat it, it's likely that someone will be hurt. "With his mouth the godless man would destroy his neighbor." Here we return to where we began. Proverbs 18:21 says, "Death and life are in the power of the tongue."

Let's conclude with a sober warning about words. Ephesians 4:29 says, "Let no corrupting talk come out of your mouths." Using curse words should probably be classified as "corrupting talk." The verse does not say, "Don't use corrupting talk unless you're by yourself and nobody can hear you." It doesn't say, "Don't use corrupting talk unless you're really angry and you know it will help you to vent." No, "Let no corrupting talk come out of your mouths." Colossians 3:8 says, "You must put them all away: anger, wrath, malice, slander, and obscene talk from your mouth." The Greek word translated "obscene talk" refers to vulgar, dirty words. The Bible says, "Put them all away."

Still, the most important message of this chapter doesn't have to do with our words. It has to do with our hearts. Remember what Jesus said? "Out of the abundance of the heart the mouth speaks." When our words are wrong, it's because our hearts are wrong. We don't need mouth surgery; we need heart surgery, and only Jesus can change our hearts. If we finish this chapter thinking that the main point is to clean up the way we talk, then we've missed the good news. The good news is that we speak wickedly because our hearts are wicked, but Jesus died on the cross for our sins and rose again, and he offers forgiveness for sin and new life to those who put their faith in him. The most important point is the condition of our hearts, and to have clean hearts we need Jesus.

When we receive Jesus by faith, he'll be in us and with us. He'll change us from the inside out by his power. One result of that change is that we'll use different patterns of speech. Right now, say to the Lord, "Lord, help me to tame my tongue. Help me to eliminate all the wicked ways of using words, and practice all the wonderful ways of using words." That's a prayer he'll answer. In fact, he has already answered it by giving us his wisdom for living well.

QUESTIONS FOR
REFLECTION

1. Make a list of persons you can encourage in the next week. What should you say to each one?

2. Are there sins you should confess or a relationship you can restore? What's keeping you from doing it right away?

3. Of the six sinful ways of using words, which are problems for you? What is your plan for correcting the problem?

CHAPTER 3

GOD'S WISDOM FOR WOMEN

IN *WHERE HAVE ALL THE MOTHERS GONE?* BRENDA HUNTER writes about the difficulty of being a mother today. A woman is expected to earn her share of the family income, do the housework, raise children on nonexistent time, look like a movie star, and be a scintillating partner to her husband. Such expectations are fueled by selfish desires and are obviously unrealistic, but they are real in our culture. Such unrealistic expectations have led many women to cynicism. They're cynical because they know it's impossible to meet all the expectations placed on them. So, they might as well live for themselves, since their family won't appreciate them anyway. Brenda Hunter expressed this common way of thinking when she wrote,

> Narcissism is the philosophy of the age. Articles and books tell us that our first responsibility is to ourselves. Don't live for family; don't allow mother feelings to curtail the pursuit of self. Our children may well mess up their lives, or at best will simply grow up and leave home, so don't

invest too much time in them. ... Husbands? They too may fail us. The escalation of divorce supports the idea that "number oneism" is all that's left. If we women do not look out for ourselves, we just may find ourselves old, divorced, unfulfilled and unemployed.[1]

In contrast with the philosophy of our times that Hunter describes, God's wisdom calls women to look out for their families and for others, not for themselves. Therefore, God's wisdom is radically different from the spirit of our times. He is the one, however, who knows how to live well. The women who follow his wisdom should be praised.

Our culture portrays femininity in a variety of ways. Familiar media images include the driven businesswoman, the sexy seductress, the Martha Stewart / Betty Crocker supermom, and the impossibly thin supermodel. Real womanhood, real femininity, doesn't fit into any of those categories. Those images exist only in the media. Watching them is like watching a movie about Harry Potter or hobbits—interesting, but we should not expect the fantasy to reflect reality.

Proverbs 31 provides a portrait of a woman that is rooted in reality. Compared to the fantasies of media femininity, it looks pretty radical, but it's also real. It's real wisdom for real women, a description of a wise, godly woman inspired by God himself. The Hebrew text of Proverbs 31:10–31 is in the form of an acrostic poem. Each line of the poem begins with a successive letter of the Hebrew alphabet, the Hebrew equivalent of A to Z. These verses were considered to be one poem, and they were meant to be read together. Let's look at this portrait and note six hallmarks of a wise woman.

WISE WOMEN PROVE THEIR FIDELITY

In God's book of wisdom, a virtuous woman is defined by fidelity to her family. The word "fidelity" summarizes

Proverbs 31:11–12. Verse 11 says, "The heart of her husband trusts in her." She's worthy of his trust. He can count on her. Why? Verse 12 answers that question: "She does him good, and not harm, all the days of her life." Trust is earned, and this wise woman who is worthy of praise has earned the trust of the man who knows her best. That requires daily fidelity. In good times and in hard times, she has been faithful, consistently doing her husband good. Notice that verse 12 says that she's faithful "all the days of her life." Year after year, she proves her faithfulness.

That's not necessarily what we see in the media. For example, Judith Warner has written a book entitled *Perfect Madness: Motherhood in the Age of Anxiety*.[2] In that book she describes motherhood as draining drudgery, and she writes that if women want self-fulfillment they should seek it *away from* their families. Caring for family involves long hours of work and stress, so if women want self-fulfillment they'll have to be free of family. The self, or what women want for themselves, stands at the center of Warner's vision.

Here is a fundamental difference between God's way of living well and the world's way of living. The world's way asks, "What can I do for me? What will make me happy?" God's way of wisdom has to do with fearing and loving him, and loving and serving others. The difference is between living for self and giving to others. God made us for something more, something bigger, than ourselves, so living for self-pleasure leads to disappointment. The writer of the book of Ecclesiastes searched for meaning by participating in all kinds of selfish pursuits, but he concluded they were all "vanity," or emptiness, without God (see, for example, Eccl 2:1–26). On the other hand, faithfully serving others leads to great joy and fulfillment. Proverbs 31:12 portrays the wise woman doing good not for herself but for her husband all the days of her life, and verse 28 says that she is blessed and praised for it.

WISE WOMEN PROVIDE
THROUGH THEIR INDUSTRY

Wise women are hard workers. I saw a sign once that said, "Hard work won't kill you, but why take the chance?" Some people have that attitude, but it's not the attitude of the wise woman described in Proverbs 31. Verses 13-19 describe the many ways in which she works. Verse 13 says, "She seeks wool and flax." Some ladies today do that on a regular basis. Before I was married, I don't know if I was aware of the existence of stores that sell fabric to make clothes. Since I've been married, I have become very aware of those stores—aware enough to know that if my wife is about to go to one of those stores, I should immediately become busy with something that is highly important so I won't have to go look at cloth. When I am in a fabric store I am the only man, and I can almost feel the testosterone draining out of my system. It's work, but it's exactly what the woman of Proverbs 31 does. She does it to provide clothes for her family and provide them at a reasonable price, because she's making the clothes herself. We know that because she is looking for fabric, not clothes.

Verse 14 says that she even travels far to get food for her family. "She is like the ships of the merchant; she brings her food from afar." Many children are not aware of all the work that's necessary to provide food for their families. Often wise mothers collect coupons by the dozens. They look for bargains, and they consider nutritional value. When they come home with the car full of groceries, they're not unlike merchant ships loaded down with cargo!

Verse 15 says the wise woman rises in the morning while it's still dark to prepare food for her family. Verses 16 and 24 state that this wise woman also has a business: she buys and sells land, plants a vineyard, and makes clothes and sells them. Verse 17 is a common biblical way to refer to work— "she dresses herself." It's an expression that refers to pulling up one's long robe and tucking it in a belt so that it will not get in the way of the work. This woman is hiking up her dress and getting to work!

Verse 27 says, "She looks well to the ways of her household," and verse 18 says, "Her lamp does not go out at night." She's up late, looking after her family. Paul wrote in Titus 2:5 for Titus to tell the older ladies in the church to instruct the younger ladies to be "working at home." That's a mark of a Christian lady who's worthy of praise. She works hard at home.

Every year, compensation experts at Salary.com, a company based in Waltham, Massachusetts, calculate the earning power of the work done by mothers. At the end of the first decade of the 21st century, those experts were estimating that a stay-at-home mother would earn about $122,732 if she were paid for her work as a housekeeper, teacher, cook, janitor, facilities manager, van driver, and psychologist. Mothers employed outside the home would earn about $76,185 for the work they do at home in addition to their employment. Obviously, mothers work very hard.[3]

I wonder if such salary computations are prepared primarily for people who don't already value the work mothers do. People who *do* value their work know that no labor is comparable to the work of mothers. What they do is not worth just $122,732 per year. It's priceless, because there is nothing more important than shaping the next generation for God and for good.

Robert Moffat was a missionary who led multitudes of people to faith in Christ. Someone once said that when Robert Moffat was added to the kingdom of God, a whole continent was added with him. It may sound strange, but he gave credit for all his missionary labors to his mother's kiss. He said that after he reached adulthood and was leaving home, his mother walked with him part of the way. When she stopped and was about to go back as he traveled on, she asked Robert to make her a promise. He said, "Before I can promise I'll have to know what I'm promising to do." His mother said, "Robert, it's something you can easily do. Promise your mother." So, he said, "Okay, Mother, I promise to do what you wish." She clasped her hands behind his head and pulled his face down to hers and said, "Robert, you're going out into a wicked world. Begin every day with God. Close every day with God." Then she kissed him and said good-bye. Robert Moffat later said it was that kiss that made him a missionary. Mothers should never underestimate the power of their godly lives and counsel.

WISE WOMEN PRACTICE GENEROSITY

Godly mothers are generous. Proverbs 31:20 says, "She opens her hand to the poor and reaches out her hands to the needy." This woman spends a lot of time and effort to provide clothes and food for her family. She's involved in the material things of life, but she's not materialistic. She considers the needs of her own family unselfishly, and she also considers the needs of the poor. Somebody said that you can always recognize a mother. If you present five pieces of pie to a group of six people, the mother will be the one who says, "No, thanks. I'm not really hungry."

Somebody sent me a list of questions about mothers that were answered by elementary schoolchildren. One question was, "What's the difference between moms and dads?" One child wrote, "Moms have magic. They make you feel better without medicine." Another question was, "What does your mom do in her spare time?" One answer was, "She doesn't do spare time." "What ingredients are mothers made of?" "God makes mothers out of clouds and angel hair and everything nice in the world, and one dab of mean." "Why did your mom marry your dad?" "My grandma says that Mom didn't have her thinking cap on." Yes, we know that a wise woman is generous. "She opens her hand to the poor, and she reaches out her hands to the needy." She's generous, industrious, and faithful.

WISE WOMEN PREPARE FOR ADVERSITY

Women who have real wisdom don't quit in adversity; they persevere. Verse 21 says, "She is not afraid of snow for her household, for all her household are clothed in scarlet." Verse 25 makes a similar point: "She laughs at the time to come." She does not fear the future because she has prepared for it. She has taken care of her family in advance. If a winter storm comes, her family won't be in danger because she has already provided plenty of warm clothing. She prepares for adversity.

Adversity is a part of life. The phony women presented in the media face phony adversity, if they face adversity at all. Real women face real adversity. Sarah, the wife of Abraham, had to deal with childlessness until she was ninety years old. In the ancient world, childlessness was viewed as a curse. It could not have been easy to be seen as cursed, but Sarah had to live with that. Her behavior was not always exemplary, but she endured and God gave her and Abraham a son (Gen 12–21). Naomi and Ruth had to grieve over the deaths of their husbands, and they fought poverty and starvation in a land where they had no home. They trusted God, and God provided (Ruth 1–4). Hannah suffered through childlessness, and she had to endure her husband having a second wife. Hannah prayed, pouring out her heart to God, and God blessed her with a son (1 Sam 1–2). Esther risked her life to rescue her people, not knowing whether she would survive. God protected her providentially and used her to save the Jewish people during the Persian period (Esth 4–7). Mary bore the stigma of pregnancy out of wedlock (Matt 1). Still, she said to the angel who announced her pregnancy to her, "Let it be to me according to your word" (Luke 1:38).

All these women, including the woman described in Proverbs 31, had to face problems. All women have difficulties, but some women put additional pressure on themselves by harboring the unrealistic expectation that if they can just do everything well enough, then everything will work out perfectly. There is a place for everything, and everything in its place. Schedules must be planned and executed perfectly. The baby is fed every four hours—not 3½ or 4½. He takes a nap at two o'clock and goes to bed at eight. Every family has certain rules about how things are to be done—don't track dirt on the carpet, use your napkin, wash behind your ears, clean up after yourself, put it back where you got it, if you turned it on turn it off. But sometimes things break, schedules don't work out, things get dirty, and people get hurt. Real women do not live problem-free, germ-free lives. They have problems. The question is, will they be prepared for problems, and will they persevere through those problems?

Wise women don't want their children to grow up to be quitters, so they don't quit. In any one of a thousand difficulties, they could have quit, but they persevered. I'm not suggesting that Proverbs teaches, "Just be wise, don't quit, and everything will work out wonderfully!" Sometimes problems don't end well. Sometimes a husband is abusive, the wife must separate for the sake of her safety, and her husband is not interested in changing or reconciling. A woman's circumstances can go south badly. But that doesn't mean that she has stopped persevering or that she has given up her faith. She can pick up the pieces and enter the next chapter trusting God and following His wisdom. Even through the worst of difficulties, wise women persevere. In this fallen world, sometimes that's as good as "living well" gets. Think of the ways persevering women have enriched the world. The world had Augustine only because Augustine had his mother, Monica. Augustine was an immoral young man, living for the moment and going from woman to woman. His Christian mother persevered in prayer for him and continued to live as an example before him, until he finally came to Christ and blessed the world by his leadership in the church and by writing books like *The City of God* and his *Confessions*. Real women face adversity. Women with real wisdom are prepared for it, and they persevere through it.

WISE WOMEN PRIORITIZE SPIRITUALITY

The priority of wise women is to fear the Lord. Proverbs 31:30 says, "Charm is deceitful, and beauty is vain, but a woman who fears the LORD is to be praised." In our society, women are constantly pressured to place great emphasis on how they look. Incessant advertisements tell them they should buy more cosmetics, more clothes, jewelry, and perfume if they want to look presentable or have any hope of looking physically attractive. Many women fall into this trap and make their appearance their priority. They spend more time arranging their makeup and hair than they spend in God's word and prayer. The focus of their minds is on their clothes and appearance. That's not wise, because "Charm is deceitful, and beauty is vain." We use the word "vain" to refer to being conceited, or self-centered. The Hebrew word translated "vain" was used to refer to a breath. In a derived sense it was used to mean "transitory," "empty," and even "worthless." "Charm is deceitful, and beauty is empty, worthless."

Why is beauty worthless? Our physical beauty fades. Our hair either turns gray or begins to fall out. Our skin wrinkles, and contrary to what Hollywood and Madison Avenue say, that's not bad—it's unavoidable; it's life. Our beauty will go away, and if we prioritize how we look, we're going to wake up one day and look into the mirror and realize that we've put our eggs in the wrong basket and prioritized the wrong thing. However, if we emphasize our relationship with God—loving him, fearing him, and knowing him—we'll become more and more beautiful each year, to other people and to God. That's exactly what Peter wrote in 1 Peter 3:3-4. Addressing ladies, he wrote, "Do not let your adorning be external—the braiding of hair and the putting on of gold jewelry, or the clothing you wear—but let your adorning be the hidden person of the heart with the imperishable beauty of a gentle and quiet spirit, which in God's sight is very precious."

The negative statement in Proverbs 31:30 has to do with the deceitfulness of charm and the emptiness of beauty, but don't miss the positive statement. Verse 30 also says, "A woman who fears the LORD is to be praised." She does not fear what others may say about the condition of her appearance; she fears what God will say about the condition of her heart. Her priority is her relationship with God and pleasing him. Obviously, such a priority does not mean that wise women vow to use no makeup or to wear only drab clothes. Why not look your best?

Wise women who prioritize spirituality have amazing influence in the lives of other people, especially the members of their own families. My mother is a wonderful example of a woman with real wisdom. One of the treasures of my life has been her prayer for me. During my growing up years, as I got ready for school and walked back and forth from my bedroom to the bathroom, I would pass by my parents' bedroom door. If that door was cracked as I got ready for school and I looked into their bedroom, I would often see my mother on her knees next to her bed praying before she left the house for work. I knew she was praying for me and for my sister as we went to school that day. Through the years, she has continued to pray for me every day. Only God knows all that he has done in my life—all that has happened and all that has not happened—in answer to my mother's prayers. I have often wondered how many temptations never were presented to me, how many calamities never occurred, because my mother was praying for me. I don't know where I would be today, I don't know *what* I would be, without the prayers of my mother.

Some women might be thinking, "Wait a minute. I have a lot of time pressure and fatigue already. I have a preschooler who is the definition of perpetual motion. I've got a teenager who's questioning the most important things we've taught him. I've got more work to do than two people can do, and on top of all that you're holding up a portrait of perfection that I am supposed to match. You're talking about perfection, and I am working on survival!"

A word of encouragement: God never calls us to do something that he doesn't enable us to do. The Holy Spirit is our helper. He fills us and enables us to live the life to which he calls us. Galatians 5:22–23 lists the fruit of the Holy Spirit. That fruit is "love, joy, peace, patience, kindness, goodness, faithfulness, gentleness, self-control." These are the character traits that should be in every Christian's life, and they come from the Holy Spirit, not from us. They're not my fruit or your fruit. They're the fruit of the Holy Spirit. He lives in us, fills us, and produces his fruit in us. Maybe your prayer time will not be on your knees early in the morning. Maybe you will pray as you drive from one place to another, as you prepare for a date, as you change a diaper, as you take your lunch break at work, or as you shop. I don't know, but I do know that God will help you, and he will use your prayers to help others.

WISE WOMEN ARE PRAISED BY THEIR FAMILIES

This last mark of a wise woman is also an encouragement. Proverbs 31:28–29 and 31 state, "Her children rise up and call her blessed; her husband also, and he praises her: 'Many women have done excellently, but you surpass them all.' ... Give her of the fruit of her hands, and let her works praise her in the gates." Wise women are worthy of commendation, and their families do not fail to offer it. Such women surpass even those who "have done excellently." They should be treated nobly, like royalty.

Every person, especially those in her family, should honor wise women—not just on Mother's Day, but on every day of the year. We should consciously reject the common idea that motherhood is something anybody can do, demeaning the calling by suggesting that if you're really intelligent or capable, then you'll work outside the home and do something of "real value." Instead, we should rise up and bless women who follow God's wisdom for living well. It's possible to follow that wisdom with or without a job outside the home, and when women live wisely, we should tell them that they have acted nobly, that they are worthy of praise. Women who work hard for their families are making the most significant, the highest, most holy contribution to society that can be made. They are shaping destiny by training the will, mind, and heart of the next generation. We should give them all the praise and honor they deserve.

Several years ago I was driving home after a speaking engagement, and I began to think about the qualities in my life that are the result of my mother's influence. A few poetic lines came to mind, and I jotted them down. Later I added more lines, and on her 75th birthday, my family had my poem framed, and we gave it to her as a gift. I entitled it, "These Were My Mother's Gifts to Me."

> A tender heart toward those I lead,
> A giving hand to those in need,
> A reverent soul on bended knee,
> These were my mother's gifts to me.
> A mind that's willing to explore,
> To ask hard questions not asked before,
> To find buried answers that others ignore,
> These Mother gave me, and so much more.
> To be taciturn 'til asked to speak,

To use my words to help the weak,
To speak for those who are right but meek,
These ways of my mother still I seek.

To receive God's gift of salvation by grace,
To open the Bible to seek his face,
To bow and pray in the secret place,
These lines Mother drew, I only trace.

To seek the peace and avoid a fight,
But to be ready to stand for what is right,
To add to each conflict not heat but light,
This Mother lived before my sight.

To those who need comfort, to give my ear,
To be slow to speak but ready to hear,
To diligently work to help far and near,
This did my mother, year after year.

God knew what he planned me to be,
So he shaped my heart on my mother's knee,
I can boast of no trait, for these came free,
These were my mother's gifts to me.

My mother truly embodied all these traits, and she gave them to me, though I embody them with many more deficiencies. I once heard a woman, when asked what a stay-at-home mom like my mother did for a living, answer, "Brain surgery. Daily, noninvasive brain surgery." She was right. That's what women do when they adopt God's wisdom for living well. They may work outside the home, or they may not, but they care for their families and make an immeasurable contribution to the next generation and to everyone around them. If you know a woman like that, especially if she's your mother, find a way to "praise her in the gates." If you have already done that, it wouldn't hurt to do it again.

I close this chapter by addressing women who seek to live by God's wisdom. Your work may not be lauded in the media or society, but you are accomplishing something of far greater importance than making news. You are molding the next generation of humanity and determining the destiny of the world. When you do it well, those who know you best will praise your greatness. Your husband will praise you in the gates, and your children will rise up and call you blessed. That praise may be less glamorous than other awards, but it is of far greater value. Who is the woman who is to be praised? She is a woman of fidelity and industry, generosity and spirituality, and she plans for adversity. May all the world say, "Give her of the fruit of her hands, and let her works praise her in the gates."

QUESTIONS FOR REFLECTION

1. Do any women you know feel pressure to conform to the images of womanhood in the media? How do they respond to that pressure?
2. What inspires and motivates a woman to prioritize loving God and serving others instead of living for self?
3. Try making a list of all the jobs your mother performed, and still performs. What should your response be to what she has done for you and others?
4. Are the women you know generous? Are you generous? How do we measure generosity?
5. How can women balance the positive desire to look their best with the even greater goal of emphasizing their relationship with God?

CHAPTER 4

GOD'S WISDOM FOR MEN

Western culture promotes a variety of ideas about masculinity. One image is the physically strong rescuer, immune to pain, virtually indestructible and aloof. Think of Sylvester Stallone, Dwayne "The Rock" Johnson, Chris Hemsworth, Arnold Schwarzenegger, or Clint Eastwood. Another image our culture shows us is the strong rescuer who is also handsome, suave, and a little better at communicating. This image calls to mind James Bond, Brad Pitt, George Clooney, or Tom Cruise. Then you have the decisive, savvy, ahead-of-the-curve, worldly-wise type, with a mysterious, almost magical knack for making money. Good examples of this type of masculinity would be Warren Buffett, Bill Gates, or Mark Zuckerberg. Another common image of masculinity is the athletic phenomenon; he's gifted, hardworking, and he's got it made with the ladies and with the finances. This is the Lebron James or Peyton Manning type. Next comes the bungling-idiot type, sort of like Ray Romano on *Everybody Loves Raymond*. His wife isn't just smarter than he is; she's so far advanced beyond him it's as if he's a lower life form. His kids are also smarter than he is, even if they're preschoolers. He's clueless, inhabiting a world created by his own imagination, and he has to be rescued. Finally, there's every other man. To the media, we're white noise, living out our uneventful, pointless lives as the backdrop against which the "real men" set the agenda and create the drama.

Most men fall into the final category. Yet, media and society images cause many men to long to be in one of the other categories, if they are to really matter. That longing has contributed to the success of dozens of cottage industries that profit from promising men that they can move into one of the cooler categories. So, men attend seminars that promise to help them become wealthy, they read books about picking up girls, or they go on rustic retreats and beat on drums, their chests, or whatever is handy, to express their masculinity. They do such things because they want to be admirable men and heroes, and Western culture defines masculine worth in terms of physical strength, athletic prowess, sexual conquest, and wealth.

God's book of wisdom defines manhood differently. And shouldn't God get to define manhood, since he created it? Genesis 1:27 says, "God created man in his own image, in the image of God he created him; male and female he created them." Gender differentiation was part of God's design from the beginning. After God created gender, and everything else, this was his conclusion: "God saw everything that he had made, and behold, it was very good" (Gen 1:31). Originally, humanity, along with everything else, was "very good." "Everything" included maleness and femaleness, since gender was part of God's design.

Men, and women, should also consider the following facts. The books of the Bible were written by men. God called

Abraham, Isaac, Jacob, and Moses—men. They were patriarchs, not matriarchs. The leaders of God's people were prophets, priests, and kings. In the New Testament, the teachers and pastors of the churches were men. God is our Father, and Jesus taught us to pray, "Our Father who is in heaven," not "Our Mother." Jesus was a man, and he is the Son of God, not the daughter of God. Real men ought to feel right at home in the church of Jesus Christ.

Does that mean that the Bible and the Christian faith are chauvinistic and women are second class? Not even close. The Bible presents a much higher view of women than contemporary secular culture. The Bible describes women hearing from God and speaking for God. Women and men have equal access to God, and equal giftedness from God. Women and men are presented as equal in worth but different in roles. Women are treasured and protected by men who are willing to fight for them. For example, the book of Judges describes the brutal rape of a woman by wicked men. In response, the men of Israel went into battle against the people who were responsible. Compare that to what happens in *our* culture when a woman is raped. Instead of being championed, if she has the temerity to file charges against the rapist she will likely be vilified publicly in court.

The point is that God's word honors the right kind of masculinity, while our culture does not value male leadership or even understand it. Dr. Meg Meeker states it well in her book *Strong Fathers, Strong Daughters*. She writes,

> Most of you out there are good men ... but you are good men who have been derided by a culture that does not care for you, that ... has ridiculed your authority, denied your importance, and tried to fill you with confusion about your role. But I can tell you that fathers change lives, as my father changed mine.[1]

Dr. Meeker is right. Fathers are not just important; they are irreplaceable.

With all the flawed messages and confusion in our culture concerning masculinity, we need help in defining what it means to be a man. We need God's wisdom. He has provided that wisdom in the book of Proverbs, and it shows us how to live well. If you are a family man, I hope this chapter will make you a better man, a better husband and father; if you are single, God's wisdom will help strengthen you for healthy family relationships—with current family members, with the family of God, and, if you marry, with your future wife and children. If you are a single woman, it will help you to know what to look for in a man if you are interested in marriage. Let's take a whirlwind tour of the book of Proverbs, noticing what it says about men. The ten principles we will encounter are found elsewhere in the Bible, but we'll look primarily at the way they're expressed in the book of Proverbs.

WISE MEN MODEL MARITAL FAITHFULNESS

Proverbs 18:22 says, "He who finds a wife finds a good thing and obtains favor from the LORD." God's book of wisdom says that it's good to find a wife, and he gives his favor to a man who finds a wife. But being a good man and a good father involves not only being a husband, but being a *good* husband. Proverbs 31:10–31 describes a wife who is virtuous, industrious, and praiseworthy. One reason the Proverbs 31 woman is so great is because she has a great husband. Some guys say, "I wish I had a wife like the woman described in Proverbs 31." But remember, this woman probably didn't become great overnight. The woman of Proverbs 31 had adult children, so she was probably in the middle years. Also, the wonder woman of Proverbs 31 had a husband who helped her. Proverbs 31:11 says that the woman's husband trusts in her. Verse 23 says that her husband is known among the elders of the city, and he sits in the gate of the city where the city leaders meet. So, the man who is married to the woman of Proverbs 31 is a man who has earned the respect of the people who know him. They have made him a leader. Verses 28–29 say that the woman's husband gives her encouragement and praise. He says, "Many women have done excellently, but you surpass them all." In other words, the model woman of Proverbs 31 had a model husband, and that husband modeled for his children how to be a good husband.

Modeling marriage for children is still important today. It's been said many times, but it's still true—the best thing men can do for their children is to love their wives. Not only does that create family stability when the children are young, but when those children grow up and marry they tend to relate to their spouses in the way they saw Mom and Dad relate to one another. Here's the principle: the perpetuation of parental patterns is probable. Acting like our parents is our default mode.

It's important to be aware that we tend to replicate parental patterns. However, it's also important to recognize that though such generational cycles are probable, they are *not* inevitable. With God's help we can break any negative behavior patterns we may have witnessed in our parents. Here's the challenge for husbands: when you're thinking about how to respond to your wife, remember that the way you respond is likely to be replicated by your son in his marriage, or your daughter is likely to look for a man who behaves like you do. It's imperative, then, for men to model marital faithfulness.

WISE MEN TAKE RESPONSIBILITY

We see just the opposite all the time. When some men get married they tell their wives, "I love you more than life itself," and yet when things get hard they quit. Proverbs 27:8 says, "Like a bird that strays from its nest is a man who strays from his home." That describes men who are irresponsible; they wander from their homes. They quit the marriage by divorce; they quit by hiding at the office, hiding at the golf course, or even hiding at church. Proverbs 12:11 refers to a man who pursues worthless things; that's the man who leaves his wife physically or emotionally. Men can quit the marriage and hide emotionally even when they're with their wives. Their wives ask them, "Things don't seem right with us, Honey; how are you? You seem distant these days." He is distant, and he feels it, but he says, "I'm fine. Nothing's wrong." He's hiding, not taking responsibility for his feelings.

Real men take responsibility for their marriages. They make them what God intends them to be, and they love their wives. A lot of guys check out of their marriages because it's hard, but being a man means taking responsibility and doing what's necessary even when it's hard. Because of the fall, *everything* is hard—except for sin. After Adam and Eve sinned, God cursed the ground so that work would be hard (Gen 3:17–19). So, following God's way after the devastating results of the fall may be hard, but Proverbs 18:9 says, "Whoever is slack in his work is a brother to him who destroys." When men don't do the hard work of taking responsibility, precious relationships are destroyed. Real men are not slackers. They take responsibility.

WISE MEN PROVIDE FOR THEIR FAMILIES

To most people in the modern West, prosperity means having money in the bank, fancy cars, boats, and lots of other stuff. That's not prosperity in the biblical sense. Men should never think, "My kids don't have as much stuff as my friend's kids, so I'm not as good a father." In the Bible, material prosperity means not having to worry about whether there is food to eat. From the perspective of the Bible, the reason families have enough is that God, in his grace, has blessed them, and Dad and Mom have worked hard to provide. First Timothy 5:8

says, "If anyone does not provide for his relatives, and especially for members of his household, he has denied the faith and is worse than an unbeliever." Even unbelievers provide for their families materially. Why would Christian men not be able to keep up with that?

Proverbs 13:22 says, "A good man leaves an inheritance to his children's children." A good man is marked by industry and frugality—he works hard, and he doesn't spend everything he makes. Historically, people have called that the "Protestant work ethic." Actually, such an ethic was in the Bible long before Protestants existed. When people read the Bible, they see that God calls us to industry and frugality. The result of working hard and saving is that wise parents have something to leave to their children and grandchildren. Even young men who are not married ought to be working toward the inheritance they will leave to their children and grandchildren, if God should so bless them. A young man should think about his future in terms of long-term stability and prosperity—spiritual, material, and emotional stability and prosperity. While other guys may wonder whether their marriage will make it or not, men who follow God's wisdom for living well *know* they're going to do what it takes to make it work, and because of that, they're planning for their grandchildren. Wise men provide for their families.

WISE MEN TRAIN THEIR CHILDREN TO BE WISE

Wise dads teach their children how to be right with God. Proverbs 22:6 is one of the most familiar verses in Proverbs: "Train up a child in the way he should go; even when he is old he will not depart from it." The original Hebrew doesn't have the word "should." The verse says simply, "Train a child according to his way," or the way that is appropriate to that child. Don't miss the main point—parents are to train their children.

The Hebrew of Proverbs 22:6 may also be translated in a way that makes the verse a warning. Remember that the verse is translated literally: "Train a child according to his way, and when he is old he will not depart from it." If "his way" is understood to be in *contrast* to God's way, then the verse refers to the kind of passive parenting that allows a child to do his or her own thing even when it contrasts with God's way or the parents' way. The parents don't interfere with the child's "natural" development for fear that they may warp his little psyche. Misbehavior is not corrected, and sometimes it is even celebrated as an expression of the child's individuality. So, the child jabs a knife into your computer keyboard—"Look! He's going to be an IT expert!" In that case, the warning of Proverbs 22:6 is that when a child is raised according to his own way, he will continue in that way. He doesn't know anything else. The child who was a pain to his parents has become an adult who is a pain to everyone.

Ephesians 6:4 says, "Fathers, do not provoke your children to anger, but bring them up in the discipline and instruction of the Lord." The New Testament describes three types of parental instruction. The first type is *moral instruction*. In Hebrews 12, the word translated "discipline" or "training" can also be translated "chastening," and it refers to God's discipline, or corrective punishment, in our lives (vv. 5, 11). In 2 Timothy 3:16 the same term is translated "instruction," or "training," in righteousness. It is positive, constructive discipline or instruction, part of training a young person to live morally. The purpose is character development. Men have the responsibility to instill moral values in their children. Wise fathers train their children to be wise—not foolish, sensual, contentious, or lazy.

Ephesians 6:4 also describes *mental instruction*. The next word in the verse is "instruction." The Living Bible (TLB) paraphrases the word as "godly advice." The Greek word translated "instruction" refers to impressing something on someone's mind, so this is mind instruction. In a few places in the New Testament the word has the meaning of teaching in order to warn. For example, Titus 3:10 states, "As for a person who stirs up division, after warning him once and then twice, have nothing more to do with him." Wise men inform and warn their children. They make sure their kids understand the consequences of sin.

The last kind of instruction Ephesians 6:4 includes is *spiritual instruction*. The discipline and instruction is "of the Lord." The context of a man's instruction is faith in the Lord. The goal of parental education is for children to know and obey God. Wise men speak of right and wrong, but they also speak of the One who determines right and wrong. We teach the consequences of sin, but we also offer the One who can deliver us from temptation. More than merely rules and warnings, we speak about Christ.

Relay races are won or lost in the transfer of the baton. Wise men work hard to pass the baton of faith and wisdom carefully to the next generation. The remainder of the child's life will be affected by the way the baton is passed. Moral and spiritual instruction is not something that men delegate to "the little woman." Real men train their children. They read and teach the Bible. They talk about Christ to the children. In Proverbs 23:17, a father says to his son, "Let not your heart envy sinners, but continue in the fear of the LORD all the day." In other words, "Son, don't feel like you have to be like other kids. Be willing to be different. Let's always fear the Lord." Wise men give that kind of spiritual training to their children.

WISE MEN ARE EXAMPLES OF MORALITY

God's book of wisdom says that wise men not only *tell* their children how to live good lives, they *show* them how to live good lives. In fact, if men are not showing such a life, they shouldn't bother telling anybody about it, because telling without showing is useless. Proverbs 26:7 says, "Like a lame man's legs, which hang useless, is a proverb in the mouth of fools." What a word picture! Of what use are legs to a guy who can't walk? He isn't using them; they're just in the way. He might as well not have them. That's what it's like for a fool to speak wise words. So, if a foolish guy picks up a wise saying somewhere, he needn't bother repeating it. Nobody's buying it, especially his kids. If he's not living a wise life, trying to speak wise words is useless. If he's not living a righteous life, teaching righteousness is pointless. Children can recognize hypocrisy before they're able to pronounce the word, so wise words are as useless to a fool as legs to a lame man.

Proverbs 20:7 says, "The righteous who walks in his integrity—blessed are his children after him." When I was about eleven years old, the men in my father's office went night fishing, and a few of them took their sons. We situated several boats close together on the lake, and we began fishing. Unfortunately, the fish weren't biting that night. Also unfortunately, some of the men brought alcohol. The more the fish didn't bite, the more they drank, and the more they drank, the more drunk they became. As their inhibitions lowered, they began to say things they may not have said otherwise. They became profane. They also poured scorn on those who were not participating with them in their drinking. The person they singled out for mocking was my father. He was "holier than thou," and "he thinks he's too good for us," they proclaimed, all because he refused to drink with them. It was inexcusable for them to speak so critically of a man in front of his son. But their scoffing had an unintended consequence. It produced respect and pride for my father in the heart of his son. In fact, I'd never felt so proud of my father as I did that night. Years later, I told him that his decision to be different from the men around him made a profound impression on my young mind. I decided that I wanted to be like that.

WISE MEN APPLY LOVING DISCIPLINE

The negative word for parental correction is punishment. The more positive word is discipline. The book of Proverbs teaches that wise parents use corporal punishment as a means to train their children. As some people have said, children should be raised with a pat on the back (when they behave wisely they need encouragement and affirmation), and when they act foolishly they need a pat a little lower on the back. Proverbs 22:15 says, "Folly is bound up in the heart of a child, but the rod of discipline drives it far from him" (compare Heb 12:7). The rod of discipline helps to remove foolishness from a child.

My mother tells me that when I was very small she had to spank me for willful disobedience virtually every day, and sometimes several times per day. For her, a one-spanking day was a good day. My parents raised me during the era when many parents were using Benjamin Spock's book *Baby and Child Care* to raise their children. Spock discouraged any form of corporal punishment. I tell people facetiously that my mother spanked me with Spock's book. Corporal punishment doesn't seem to have damaged me; I'm quite sure it helped me. In fact, I hardly remember it; my parents disciplined me when I was young, and I generally respected and obeyed them as an older child and teenager. Also, as I became older, my parents changed their form of discipline to target my heart and will rather than my backside.

Proverbs 23:13-14 says, "Do not withhold discipline from a child; if you strike him with a rod, he will not die. If you strike him with the rod, you will save his soul from Sheol." The Old Testament writers use the word "Sheol" to refer either to death in general or to the place of punishment in death—hell. What does corporal punishment have to do with whether a child goes to heaven or hell? First, the rod of discipline helps to remove foolishness, and it's foolish to turn from God and toward hell. Second, corporal punishment communicates a message of respect for authority and respect for the consequences for wrongdoing. Authority and consequences are very important lessons for children to learn, because they're part of life. When Daddy says not to touch the stove, if the child touches the stove anyway, his hand is burned. When the law says not to drive over sixty miles an hour on this road, if the teen does it anyway, he experiences the consequences. When God says every person is a sinner and needs Christ in order to be reconciled to him and go to heaven, the consequence for not doing that is hell. In each of those cases, the difference between happy living and suffering is respect for authority. God's book of wisdom says that when we teach our children respect for authority and respect for the consequences of wrongdoing by using the rod, we will deliver them from far worse suffering.

Wise parents apply physical discipline with love and instruction, not anger. Proverbs 3:12 says, "The LORD reproves him whom he loves, as a father the son in whom he delights." God corrects us because he loves us. This verse provides an analogy for God's loving correction—the image of a father. The writer of this proverb assumed that his readers would know that a father disciplines his son because he loves him and delights in him. And the writer is attempting to communicate that God disciplines us for the same reason.

"The rod of discipline" has become unpopular in many circles today. For example, a judge ruled in favor of a twelve-year-old girl in Quebec who challenged her father after he did not allow her to go on a school trip. Her father grounded her because she had posted inappropriate pictures of herself online using a friend's computer. Those transgressions were part of a list of rules the girl had broken, but a court sided with her and reversed the parental punishment.[2] A county court in Minnesota found a father guilty of abusing his son because he spanked him. Child protective services took the son out of the home for six months until the decision was reversed on appeal. The son told the *Minneapolis Star Tribune* the following about his parents: "They didn't, like, abuse us or anything. I was a really bad kid. ... I understand now that my dad paddled me because he loves me, and he wants me to have success in my life. He disciplined me; he didn't abuse me. They're very different things."[3] They *are* very different things. The discipline described in the Bible is applied out of love, not anger; and it is to help children, not to hurt them. Wise men know the difference, and they apply loving discipline.

WISE MEN GUARD THEIR CHILDREN'S PURITY

Proverbs 1:8-10 records a parental warning about the dangers of participating in sin. Verse 10 says, "My son, if sinners entice you, do not consent." In other words, "Son, don't go along with the crowd. Don't be a part of that wild group of guys." Proverbs 5 has the words of a father to a son warning him about sensual women. The father describes sensual women to the son, and he tells the son, "Stay away from them."

Deuteronomy 22:13-18 says that in Israel if a man married a woman and then claimed that she was not a virgin when he married her, the woman's parents were to go to the elders, and her father was to speak on her behalf and bring evidence of her virginity. Obviously, doing that required the father to know about his daughter's purity and to be willing to defend it publicly. If a young lady has any kind of relationship with a young man, her father ought to know him well, and he ought to know what they are doing together. If Dad is not going to hold his children accountable to live a pure life, who's going to do it? Their friends? Not likely. Our culture? No way. Somebody has to step up and take responsibility. Why not Dad?

The church can help men with this. Many churches rally parents and their children to use "True Love Waits" or another program to challenge their teenagers to commit themselves to purity. We participated in such programs with our children. Plus, I planned special times away from home when I talked about sexual purity with our sons, and my wife did the same with our daughter. We and our children signed the "True Love Waits" commitment card, and we put it on our refrigerator so they could see it every day.

Our older son committed to sexual purity in the "True Love Waits" program when he was about fourteen years old. One way the organization promoted that program in those days was to take a copy of all the commitment cards that had been signed by teenagers all over the country, attach them to little sticks, and place them in the ground around the convention center at the annual meeting of the denomination that sponsored the program. The year our son signed his card, approximately 250,000 commitment cards were in the ground all around that arena. As we walked into the convention center one day, our son decided that he wanted to find the card he had signed. So, he and my wife got down on their knees and started looking for his card. I couldn't believe what I was seeing. I thought, "This is impossible! Surely they have better sense than to think they can find one card among 250,000." The convention was in Orlando, and it was June. I was standing there in a suit and tie, and I was starting to sweat. I told my wife and son, "Guys, get a grip; there are 250,000 cards here!" I started doing the math and telling them that with two of them working steadily it would take about ten hours to look at half those cards. Just at that moment, my son said, "Here it is." And there it was. Against all the odds, he found his card. We took a picture to capture the moment. Finding the card he had signed to commit to purity meant a lot to him. Today, looking back on my impatience with him and my wife, I realize how foolish I was. At that moment, showing my son that I shared his commitment and excitement was much more important than my discomfort or getting to the convention. I should have known that. All men should know that. We men should know how important it is to be committed to our children's purity.

WISE MEN PRACTICE AND TEACH DILIGENCE

The book of Proverbs is a repository of wisdom to be passed from one generation to the next. A major part of that wisdom is the wisdom of work. Proverbs 14:23 says, "In all toil there is profit, but mere talk tends only to poverty." Children are naturally lazy and interested in doing only what they want to do. In fact, *adults* are naturally lazy and interested in doing only what they want to do. One difference between foolishness and wisdom is that wise people accept the fact that sometimes they have to do things they don't want to do even when it's difficult. The difficulty is what makes it work; if it were easy, it would be play! Being a wise man involves willingness to work.

Consider the following proverbial illustration about work:

> Go to the ant, O sluggard;
> consider her ways, and be wise.
> Without having any chief,
> officer, or ruler,
> she prepares her bread in summer
> and gathers her food in harvest.
> How long will you lie there, O sluggard?
> When will you arise from your sleep?
> A little sleep, a little slumber,
> a little folding of the hands to rest,
> and poverty will come upon you like a robber,
> and want like an armed man. (Prov 6:6–11)

The wisdom teacher instructed his students to watch the ants. Ants are always working. If ants are anything, they're diligent. They don't take a day off; they don't take vacations; they don't even take a break. If they or their families don't have enough to eat, it's not for lack of trying. They're always going somewhere as fast as their little ant legs will carry them. Ant language has no way to say, "Take this job and shove it." God's book of wisdom says that if we don't learn the lesson of the ant, we'll have to experience the consequence—poverty. Young people worry about whether they will be able to get a good job. A wise man teaches the next generation that hard workers will always have a job. Wise men instruct children about the importance of diligence.

WISE MEN WARN ABOUT IMMORALITY

The wisdom teacher of the book of Proverbs not only provided instruction about right and wrong, he also warned about the *consequences* of doing wrong. The first chapter of Proverbs vividly portrays a scene in which people involved in sin try to entice others to sin with them. "Come with us!" they say, "We shall find all precious goods ... throw in your lot among us" (1:11, 13-14). The wise man tells the naive young person, "Do not walk in the way with them; hold back your foot from their paths" (v. 15). We can almost hear the tempted young person respond, "But why? What's so bad about getting rich?" The wise man replies, they "lie in wait for their own blood; they set an ambush for their own lives" (v. 18). The consequence of immorality is a ruined life. *That's* the reason to stay away from sin.

Another example of warning is Proverbs 5:1-5:

My son, be attentive to my wisdom;
incline your ear to my understanding,
that you may keep discretion,
and your lips may guard knowledge.

For the lips of a forbidden woman drip honey,
and her speech is smoother than oil,
but in the end she is bitter as wormwood,
sharp as a two-edged sword.
Her feet go down to death;
her steps follow the path to Sheol.

The enticements of the adulteress make adultery seem so appealing, but the consequences are bitterness and death. So, the teacher says, "Think about the consequences *before* you commit adultery!"

A similar warning is in Proverbs 23:17-21. Verse 17 has the exhortation, "Let not your heart envy sinners." Why not? Verse 21 gives the answer: "The drunkard and the glutton will come to poverty." Again, the wise man was warning young people to stay away from immorality because of the consequences.

WISE MEN ENJOY A LEGACY

Proverbs 23:24 says, "The father of the righteous will greatly rejoice; he who fathers a wise son will be glad in him." The happiest thing in my life other than my relationships with God and my wife is the knowledge that our adult children know God, serve him faithfully, and are making wise choices. Our sons are good husbands and fathers. They are moral men. They are hard workers. They serve their families, others, and their churches. They are wise men. Proverbs 10:1 says, "A wise son makes a glad father." The word translated "glad" can also mean "rejoice." I am definitely rejoicing. By God's grace, I'm beginning to enjoy a legacy.

In Proverbs 23:15-16, a man addressed his son and wrote, "My son, if your heart is wise, my heart too will be glad. My inmost being will exult when your lips speak what is right." "My inmost being" translates a Hebrew idiom that may seem odd to people today. The Hebrew word is literally "kidneys." Yes, this dad wrote that when his son spoke what is right, his kidneys rejoiced. That may be a new picture for modern readers, but it's not very different from saying, "My heart leaped within me," or "I could hardly breathe." Such statements are idiomatic acknowledgements that strong emotions have an immediate effect on our bodies. That's what the dad of Proverbs 23:16 was writing: "Son, when I see the man you have become, when I watch your upright life and hear your wise words, I feel joy deep in my gut."

A CONCLUSION

This chapter has encouraged men to step up and be men— not the way Western culture defines men, but the way God's book of wisdom defines men. The truth is that even the infinitesimally small number of superstars and billionaires are still just men. They need God's wisdom. We all do. The question is whether we will access it and apply it.

Some people may read this chapter and feel disappointment. They may have fathers who were unfaithful or were not really there for them. Some people have fathers who were abusive. Even after those children become adults, it still hurts. On the other hand, some parents provided godly examples and instruction, but their children strayed from God and have lived foolishly. Such parents typically feel great pain. Thank God, he helps such hurting children and parents. David wrote in Psalm 27:10, "My father and my mother have forsaken me, but the LORD will take me in." When Dad or Mom are far from perfect, we can look to God as the perfect Father, the heavenly Father. He will take us up like lambs in his arms and care for us. He adopts us when we turn to him in faith through Christ. Writing of Christ, the Apostle John wrote, "To all who did receive him, who believed in his name, he gave the right to become children of God" (John 1:12). Once we're in God's family, He helps us by giving His wisdom and empowering us to follow it. When we heed our heavenly Father's wisdom for living well, we become radically better fathers and mothers, sons and daughters.

QUESTIONS FOR REFLECTION

1. Do any men you know feel pressure to conform to the images of manhood in the media? How do they respond to that pressure?

2. What have been the primary models of marriage in your life? How have those models affected you?

3. How do you define prosperity? Why and how should men provide prosperity for their families?

4. What does it take for a man to train persons in the next generation in wise living, including things like moral living and diligent working?

PART TWO:
LIVING WELL
IN OUR HEARTS

CHAPTER 5

THE FOOLISHNESS OF ANGER

In 1970, the New Orleans Saints were having a poor season. By November 8, they had won one game, lost five, and tied one. On November 8, the play-off bound Detroit Lions came to New Orleans. To the surprise of many people, it was a close game. Then, Errol Mann of the Lions nailed an eighteen-yard field goal with only eleven seconds left in the game. The Lions were ahead 17–16. After the kickoff, the Saints ran one play, and it was a complete pass from quarterback Billy Kilmer to Al Dodd. Only two seconds were left in the game, and the Saints were on their own thirty-seven-yard line. Many people in the crowd that day must have been astonished when the Saints called on their kicker, Tom Dempsey, to kick a field goal. That was in the days when the goal in the NFL was on the goal line, not behind the end zone, so this was going to be a sixty-three-yard field goal. But Tom Dempsey made that sixty-three-yard field goal with only a few feet to spare, winning the game 19–17 and setting a record that still stands, almost five decades later.

I know a man who was at that game but didn't see Dempsey's field goal. He is a big fan of the Saints, and he also has a temper. Throughout the game, this man had been angry at the Saints for squandering scoring opportunities, and when the Lions made that field goal with eleven seconds left, my friend became so angry that he stomped out of the stadium. He was in the parking lot when he heard the stadium erupt with cheering, and only later did he learn what had happened. He missed one of the great athletic achievements of his lifetime because of anger. Every day, anger causes someone to miss something good and to do things that are foolish.

A man received a text message from his wife that read,

> Honey, I've been so careless. I backed your new truck into the garage door. The garage door is demolished, and your truck is badly damaged. I'm afraid that in the process I also ran your truck into your Mercedes, doing a lot of damage to both. But I'm so glad you love me and you'll forgive me. P.S. Your girlfriend called.

That woman was angry. Women may express their anger differently than men, but anger is a problem for both men and women. The old saying "Hell hath no fury like a woman scorned" may not be theologically accurate, but it does express the fact that women can feel fury and can express it violently. Everybody struggles with anger at some point, but anger rarely has done anything good for anybody.

When was the last time you were angry? What makes you angry? How do you handle your anger? Some people think that anger is not really a problem for them—except for when someone cuts them off in traffic, or when their preschooler disobeys for the fifth time in a row, or when a kid at school makes fun of them, or when the umpire makes a bad call. We *do* feel emotion at such times, and the emotion is not happiness.

Anger is not always a sin. It's an emotion, but the cause of our anger and how we handle it usually determines whether or not it's a sin. In this chapter, we'll look in God's book of wisdom to find four actions we should take to prevent sinful anger.

ACKNOWLEDGE THE DANGERS OF ANGER

Anger is dangerous. When it swirls inside us, it's like acid that corrodes our spirits and can even destroy us. God's book of wisdom warns us of such dangers, and understanding the dangers motivates us to handle our anger in a way that will deliver us from harm.

Here's the first danger: *anger causes strife*. Proverbs 15:18 says, "A hot-tempered man stirs up strife, but he who is slow to anger quiets contention." We often assume that anger is the *result* of strife—we have an argument, and we get angry. Anger is also the *cause* of strife. If conflict exists between two people, adding anger is like pouring gasoline on a fire.

Proverbs 20:3 says, "It is an honor for a man to keep aloof from strife, but every fool will be quarreling." Any fool can stumble into an argument and speak his mind, but the Bible says that *avoiding* strife is the honorable thing to do. Foolish people walk into strife; wise people walk around it. Since anger causes strife, wise people also know that handling anger is part of walking around strife.

Proverbs 29:22 adds an important reality: "A man of wrath stirs up strife, and one given to anger causes much transgression." He *causes much* transgression. Have you ever seen someone who seems to have conflict with people regularly? Do you think, "How sad. Trouble just seems to follow that poor guy." Probably not. It's more likely that he faces tense situations occasionally, like everyone, but he gets *angry*. The anger stirs up strife and causes him to abound in transgression. More anger, more strife. More anger, more transgression.

Instead of responding to tension with anger, why not respond according to Proverbs 15:1? "A soft answer turns away wrath, but a harsh word stirs up anger." If we want to end an argument, usually we can. We can respond to someone with a gentle, loving statement. It takes two to argue, and if we refuse to argue, the argument will be cancelled for lack of a quorum. We'll be at peace with other people. That's the goal, since Romans 12:18 says, "If possible, so far as it depends on you, live peaceably with all." Living "peaceably with all" is the goal, but that's hard to do if we're angry. As Golda Meir once said, "You cannot shake hands with a clenched fist."[1] The Bible says, "A hot-tempered man stirs up strife." God's will for our relationships is peace, but anger causes strife.

Second, *anger is unhealthy.* Proverbs 14:30 says, "A tranquil heart gives life to the flesh, but envy makes the bones rot." The NASB renders "envy" as "passion." The Hebrew word had both connotations. A familiar story from the book of Genesis relates that Joseph dreamed that he would rule over his brothers. After Joseph shared his dream with his brothers, they hated him so much they wanted to kill him. The Hebrew word translated "envy" is used to describe their feelings toward Joseph (Gen 37:11). Evidently, that word was used to refer to intense emotions. Proverbs 14:30 says that kind of passion makes the bones rot.

Have you ever felt unusually tired at the end of a day, and you didn't know why? At the end of some days I feel completely drained, and I think, "Why am I so tired? I don't think I worked as hard as I usually work, but I'm worn out." Then I remember that I became emotionally involved in something during the day. That passion took a toll on me physically. Psychologists have found that anger even over small things can be detrimental to our health. Anger over a traffic jam, a flat tire, a broken shoelace, or trying to find a parking place can have negative physical effects. When we're angry, all sorts of physical symptoms occur. Our heart rate quickens, our blood pressure rises, our bodies release the powerful drug adrenaline into the blood stream, and our muscles become tense. Someone has well said, "Every time we become angry, we drive a nail into our coffins."

An old fable tells of a young lion and a wildebeest went to the same water hole to quench their thirst. Arriving at the same time, they began to argue about who would drink first. Soon, they became so angry that both of them were determined to resist the other to the death. When they stopped their fighting long enough to catch their breath, they looked up and saw vultures circling overhead waiting for their death. Their quarrel was quickly resolved. Anger is like that; it only leads to an earlier death. What does God's book of wisdom say? "A tranquil heart gives life to the flesh, but envy makes the bones rot."

We should acknowledge a third danger: *anger is foolish.* Proverbs 14:17 says, "A man of quick temper acts foolishly." That is, someone who is apt to fly off the handle is foolish. I've often heard the old saying, "People who fly into a rage never make a good landing." We often refer to bursts of anger as "losing our temper." That's a strange idiom. I would love to lose my temper; the problem is that I keep finding it. Amazingly, some people excuse losing their temper. They say things like, "It's just the Irish in me," or "I've got red hair," or "That's the kind of family I was raised in." Some people even brag about their anger.

God does not attribute anger to heredity, and he doesn't laugh it off. He says that a quick-tempered man is foolish. In fact, Proverbs 29:20 asks, "Do you see a man who is hasty in his words? There is more hope for a fool than for him." If a person's temper causes him to speak before thinking, the Bible says that he has to improve to come up to the level of a fool. Acknowledge the dangers of anger—it causes strife, it's unhealthy, and it's foolish.

PREVENT THE DESCENT OF ANGER

Ephesians 4:26–32 helps us understand the way anger works.[2] First of all, verses 26–27 state, "Do not let the sun go down on your anger, and give no opportunity to the devil." When we feel anger, we should deal with it quickly; if we don't deal with it quickly we're giving the devil an opportunity. When a person is angry and doesn't resolve it that day with the Lord's help, he or she is saying, "Come on in, Mr. Demon, you're welcome in my life; here is a place for you." That place of anger becomes the foul nest where some demon will hatch all sorts of evil eggs. When terrorists plot an attack on American soil, first someone has to allow them into the country. Then they set up a base of operations and work with others in a terrorist cell to prepare for their attack. When we have anger that we don't put away quickly, we're allowing the devil entry into our lives and giving him an opportunity to form a cell of spiritual terrorism. Once he's in, he will attack and wreak all sorts of havoc.

Ephesians 4 helps us see how the devil attacks once he has a foot in the door. Verse 31 has six words that describe the deadly descent anger causes in our spirits. The first word is *bitterness*. It refers to "all bitterness" as something we should "put away." The church father Tertullian lived and ministered in the second and third centuries. Tertullian made much of the word "all," and so should we. He wrote,

> When praying the father, you are not to be angry with a brother. ... For what sort of deed is it to approach the peace of God without peace? How will he appease his Father who is angry with his brother, when from the beginning "all anger" is forbidden us?[3]

In other words, since *all* anger is forbidden, how can we possibly please God if we have *any* anger? "Put away" all anger.

Hebrews 12:15 refers to a "root of bitterness" in our hearts. The root of bitterness is an internal feeling that we have been wronged. Someone did something to us that he should not have done, or said something he should not have said, and we get that "I've been wronged" feeling. That's where anger starts, but if we listen to Hebrews 12:15, we won't let it go any further, because this passage tells us that if the root of bitterness springs up it will cause trouble and many will be defiled. Virtually every time I have spoken on the subject of bitterness, people have come to me and expressed that they have struggled to put bitterness away. So many people carry bitterness in their hearts because a friend or loved one hurt them, and they struggle to forgive. We *must* forgive, because the alternative is bitterness, and that gives the devil an opportunity in our lives.

The next word in Ephesians 4:31 is *wrath*. The NIV has the word "rage." Let's admit it—we all know what it means to boil under the surface. Anger is smoldering. It's hot and getting hotter, like a tea kettle that hasn't boiled over yet.

When we allow the devil to enter our hearts and occupy a cell in our spirits, he isn't finished with us. The next word in Ephesians 4 is *anger*. This word refers more to what happens on the outside. Hot anger has risen to the surface and has boiled over. Now we can *see* anger in the redness of the face, the tightening of the lips, and the squinting of the eyes. The wrath that was smoldering is now flaming up. Do you see how anger is getting progressively worse? This is what happens when we give the devil an opportunity; anger and its effects keep progressing. It's bad enough to feel angry on the inside, but it's even worse when we allow that anger to continue to burn until we express it. Through the years, I've written a few angry letters. I regret writing only one, and that was the one I sent. There's a big difference between feeling anger and expressing anger.

Next, verse 31 has the word *clamor*, or brawling. Here Paul is referring to loud, angry speech. Acts 23:9 says that the Pharisees and Sadducees "contended sharply" with one another over the Apostle Paul, and "a great clamor arose." The word translated "clamor" is the word used in Ephesians 4:31. When we're angry, we become louder. One Sunday, a pastor was preaching very loudly, and a little boy asked his mother, "What's he so mad at God about?" He knew that when we become angry we're louder.

So, anger that started as bitterness has now come to the surface, and the next word is *slander*. The King James Version (KJV) has "evil speaking." Now anger has progressed so that not only is our speech loud, but it's also evil. We begin to say things we don't mean—slanderous words—even to those we love. "You're a bad child," "You'll never amount to anything," "I wish I had never married you," and even, "I hate you." We say all sorts of cruel, cutting things in anger when we don't even mean them, and we know when we're saying them that they aren't true, but our unresolved anger has given the devil an opportunity. We're on a roll, and a demon says, "Yeah, and tell him this too!" And we do it because we allowed the devil into our lives, and he formed his terrorist cell. Bitterness has turned into wrath that has burst into anger, followed by clamor and slander.

Finally, the sixth word in Ephesians 4:31 is *malice*. Malice is the desire to hurt someone, the feeling that we want to see someone suffer harm. What a hideous, sinful thought that is. Jesus said,

> You have heard that it was said to those of old,
> "You shall not murder; and whoever murders
> will be liable to judgment." But I say to you that

everyone who is angry with his brother will be
liable to judgment. (Matt 5:21–22)

Jesus said that not just the act of killing, but the malicious
thought is sin. Anger can lead to such malicious thoughts.
We can actually begin to think about someone suffering harm.
According to Jesus, such a thought is sin. While such thoughts
are going through our minds, guess who is over in a corner
with a big smile on his face? Yes, it's the demon who is there
because we opened the door and let him in when we let the
sun go down on our anger.

A first- or second-century Christian document typically
called "The Shepherd, or Pastor, of Hermas" was considered
highly important by many early Christians; in this document,
the author addresses the subject of anger and refers at length
to the progression of sinful anger and its demonic origin.
The author says:

> The Lord dwells in long-suffering, but the devil
> in anger. The two spirits, then, when dwelling
> in the same habitation, are at discord with each
> other, and are troublesome to that man in whom
> they dwell. For if an exceedingly small piece of
> wormwood be taken and put into a jar of honey,
> is not the honey entirely destroyed, and does
> not the exceedingly small piece of wormwood
> entirely take away the sweetness of the honey,
> so that it no longer affords any gratification to its
> owner, but has become bitter, and lost its use? ...
> Patience is sweeter than honey, and useful to
> God, and the Lord dwells in it. But anger is bit-
> ter and useless. Now, if anger be mingled with
> patience, the patience is polluted. ... How wicked
> is the action of anger, and in what way it over-
> throws the servants of God by its action, and

turns them from righteousness. ... For nothing at all the man or woman becomes embittered on account of occurrences in their daily life, as for instance on account of their food, or some superfluous word that has been uttered, or on account of some friend, or some gift or debt, or some such senseless affair. ... Anger is foolish, and fickle, and senseless. Now, of folly is begotten bitterness, and of bitterness anger, and of anger frenzy. This frenzy, the product of so many evils, ends in great and incurable sin. For when all these spirits dwell in one vessel in which the Holy Spirit also dwells, the vessel cannot contain them, but overflows. The tender Spirit, then, not being accustomed to dwell with the wicked spirit, nor with hardness, withdraws from such a man. ... Then, ... the man is emptied of the righteous Spirit; and being henceforward filled with evil spirits, he is in a state of anarchy in every action, being dragged hither and thither by the evil spirits, and there is a complete darkness in his mind as to everything good. This, then, is what happens to all the angry.[4]

The author described the problem as common, spiritual in nature, and deadly serious. Since every person experiences this problem, and since it is so harmful to our spiritual and physical health, we need help to overcome it. We need God's wisdom to escape the powerful feelings and actions of anger.

HANDLE ANGER WISELY

The good news is that we don't have to be conquered by anger. Instead, we can conquer anger. Proverbs 16:32 says, "Whoever is slow to anger is better than the mighty, and he who rules his spirit than he who takes a city." God doesn't intend for anger to rule us. Through his presence with us and in us, he wants to help us rule our spirits.

How do we rule our spirits? How do we defeat anger? Some people say that we should just *express* it. Vent the feelings we have inside. Let it out, just say what we think, and we'll feel better afterward. Actually, that's foolish. We've just seen how the devil can use expressed anger to harm us and the people around us. A moral difference exists between expressed anger and anger that is only felt. A sinful deed is worse than a sinful thought. I would much prefer that someone *think* about killing me instead of actually killing me. The same is true with anger. Unexpressed anger is not good; expressed anger is worse.

On the other hand, some people say that we should *repress* anger. Don't express it; don't even acknowledge it. Ignore it. Pretend it isn't there. However, repressing anger is like taking a trash can full of paper, putting it in a closet, setting it on fire, closing the door, and saying, "It's not there." But it *is* there. Pretending it isn't there won't make it go away. The fire in the trash can will either burn the closet or burn down the house. The anger in our spirits will either harm our spirits or harm everything in our lives.

So what are we supposed to do when we get angry? God's word does not teach us to express sinful anger or to repress it, but to *confess* it to God. Here's what happens when we confess: First, *we speak to God.* Admit the anger is there. Tell God, "I've got some bad feelings right now. I'm beginning to feel bitterness and to burn with anger. I know that's not from you, and it's not pleasing to you." It's amazing how such a prayer will change the way we feel. It has a powerfully positive effect on our emotions, and God answers such a prayer by making his help available to us. When we speak to God like that, we're slowing down anger's demonic descent into clamor and slander. Some people say to count to ten; it's much better to speak to God.

Second, to handle anger wisely, *we slow down the process*. In order to defeat anger, we have to confess it, and we have to control it. Slowing down the process is taking control. Proverbs 14:29 says, "Whoever is slow to anger has great understanding." If we'll slow down, God will give us understanding. Slowing down gives us time to think. We have time to ask a question like, "Do I really think that the long-term outcome of expressing my anger will be positive?" Usually the answer to that question will be "Probably not." And the rule about expressing our anger is "when in doubt, don't."

Slowing down also gives us time to pray. When we pray, we remind ourselves that God is watching our behavior. Surely, thinking of his watchful eye will help to constrain any expression of anger. Surely, we don't want to displease him. Praying also accesses God's help. When we pray for God's help, he gives us strength that is beyond ourselves, and that strength enables us to control our anger.

We speak to God, we slow down the process, then *we stop expressing anger*. Just stop it. Proverbs 29:11 says, "A fool gives full vent to his spirit, but a wise man quietly holds it back." The verb is a fascinating Hebrew word; it means "to make calm." A wise man makes his spirit calm. A wise man controls his temper, but a fool loses his temper. Never say, "I can't control my temper," because you're saying that you're a fool. You *can* control your temper; we do it all the time. For example, you're in one of those heated family discussions—faces are getting red, voices are getting loud, fingers are pointing, and then the phone rings. You say in your sweetest, happiest voice, "Hellooooo. We're doing just great, Pastor! How are *you* doing?" What have you just done? You have controlled your temper.

We can control our anger. Think about this scenario that is all too common: A husband becomes angry at his wife because of something she says to him or the way she says it. He raises his voice and speaks to her in anger. The next day at the office something happens that angers him, and he doesn't express his anger. "Express my anger at work? Are you kidding? That would be unprofessional, and it would jeopardize my career!" The sad fact is that his behavior at work proves that he *can* control his anger. He chose to control it at work, but he chose not to control it when he was with those who are most important in his life. What does that say about his priorities? It's likely that he should confess sinful priorities and say to God, "With your help I want to be different around the people who matter most in my life."

We do need God's help. Galatians 5:19-21 lists the sinful deeds of the flesh. One of those sins is "fits of anger." The next verses list the fruit of the Holy Spirit. The fruit of the Spirit includes the following: "love, joy, peace, patience ... self-control." The Holy Spirit in us can produce the fruits of patience and self-control. It's a paradox. It's called "self-control," but we don't do it by ourselves. We have the help of God's Holy Spirit. Practically speaking, it works. When we feel the heat of anger rising, we say, "God, I'm getting angry right now. Please give me the patience and self-control that only you can give. Right now I feel the strength of the flesh; please fill me with your Holy Spirit and give me your divine strength in place of my puny human strength."

DEVELOP RIGHTEOUS ANGER

The first part of Ephesians 4:26 says, "Be angry and do not sin." Some anger is not sin. If all anger is sin, then Jesus was a sinner, because the Bible says that he became angry. The third chapter of Mark says that Jesus confronted some Pharisees with their wrong thinking about a man being healed on the

Sabbath. Mark 3:5 says, "He looked around at them with anger, grieved at their hardness of heart." Jesus wasn't angry because someone had done something wrong to him, but because someone else had been wronged. An injustice had been done. His was righteous anger.

It may be rare for fallen people like us to have anger that is truly righteous, but it is possible. Anger doesn't have to be the opposite of love. It can be an expression of love. When we see people being hurt and we have the unselfish impulse that it's wrong, that's righteous anger. Wife abuse should anger us. If everyone felt anger about it, surely more wife beaters would be arrested and prosecuted. World hunger should anger us. Enough food is available to feed all the children of the world, if only corrupt people would cooperate and get the food to them. Drunk driving should anger us, as it angered the mothers who founded MADD—Mothers Against Drunk Driving. Human traffickers ought to anger us. They kidnap innocent young men and women, abuse their bodies, and sell them. They're inflicting deep wounds on the bodies and souls of young people, and we ought to be angry enough to work to stop it. Pornographers ought to make us angry. They talk about First Amendment rights like they fought at Valley Forge, but all they want is a license to become rich from the filth they pour into homes—filth that corrupts minds and destroys families. It ought to anger us that babies are being killed in the wombs of their mothers because they're too expensive, too embarrassing, or too inconvenient. It should anger us that the fathers of those babies refuse to take responsibility to care for them and raise them.

Some things *ought* to make us angry. That doesn't mean that we'll have a mean spirit and be bitter toward people. Is it possible to hate what someone does and love them? Sure it is. I hate a lot of things that I do, but I don't hate myself. It's the same way with our children. When we see them do things that could hurt them or destroy their lives, we feel anger. We feel angry not because we hate them but because we love them.

So, we ought to hate sin, but Jesus didn't say that people would know us as his disciples by our righteous anger. He said, "By this all people will know that you are my disciples, if you have love for one another" (John 13:35). First Corinthians 13 says that love "is patient. ... not irritable or resentful." It also says that love "does not rejoice at wrongdoing, but rejoices with the truth" (vv. 4–6). So, love is rarely expressed as anger, and we ought always to love. When we submit to Jesus as Lord, he helps us to heed his wisdom for living well, to express love, and to handle foolish anger his way.

QUESTIONS FOR
REFLECTION

1. Has anger ever been a problem for you? Do you still struggle with controlling your anger?
2. What negative consequences of anger have you witnessed in your life or in others' lives?
3. When we feel anger rising, what steps should we take immediately to prevent the expression of sinful anger?
4. How can we have righteous anger over wrongdoing while expressing love to wrongdoers?

CHAPTER 6

THE STRANGE DISEASE OF PRIDE

IN THE FIRST DECADE OF THE 21ST CENTURY, THE TELEVISION show *American Idol* was a runaway success. The initial episode in 2008 was viewed by 33.2 million people, over 10 percent of the population of the United States.[1] The show was a cultural phenomenon, broadcast in over one hundred countries outside the United States.[2] Some people watched to see who would win, while others were interested in seeing just how bad some of the contestants were. Some of the contestants truly could not sing, but they didn't *know* they could not sing. When the judges told them how bad they sounded, many contestants were genuinely astonished, and sometimes even angry that anyone would claim they could not sing.

The "American idol" was supposed to be the winner of the competition. It's sad but true that a lot of people idolized the winners. This chapter addresses another sad but true fact: a lot of Americans idolize themselves—they are their own idols.

God's way is different. He says, "You shall have no other gods before me" (Exod 20:3). Pride inevitably makes self into a god, our own little idol. Yet, only one true God exists. If we're wise, we'll destroy our idols and worship that one true God.

Pride is a disease that makes us unwell in numerous ways. One consequence of pride is the delusion that exaggerates our abilities and camouflages our weaknesses. To one degree or another, pride deceives all of us in just that way. We are all fallen people. Spiritually speaking, we were all born without talent. Pride prevents us from seeing the truth about our sin. Pride is spiritually deadly, but it's also difficult to detect, and the more pride we have the less likely we are to see it. Someone has said that pride is a strange disease; it makes everyone sick except for the one who has it.

Pride is especially difficult for Christians to recognize, since we can even become proud of our humility. I once heard about a monk who was bemoaning the fact that his order of monks was not as famous for scholarship as were the Jesuits, and not as famous for silence and good works as were the Trappists. "But," he said, "When it comes to humility, we're tops."

Pride can be so difficult to detect, but so deadly to our spirits. Therefore, examining our hearts for pride and then eliminating it are essential practices in living a wise life. Let's begin by stating what pride is *not*. Rejoicing in receiving an honor is not necessarily sinful pride. For example, when students are happy to make straight As, or athletes are happy to receive a trophy, they don't necessarily have sinful pride. Satisfaction in a job well done is not necessarily pride at all. We *ought* to do a good job and be glad that we did, as long as we don't think that we're superior because of it or look down on others because their work may not be of the same quality. Colossians 3:23 says, "Whatever you do, work heartily, as for the Lord and not for men." Whatever we do, we ought to do our best, not because of pride but because we do it for the

Lord, and he deserves the best. If we are sweeping the floor, we ought not to miss the corners; we're doing it for the Lord.

Also, wealth is not the same as pride. Some people assume that everybody who is wealthy is proud. Wealth comes with the temptation to be proud, but rich people can be humble, and many are. Pride is not external or material. Pride is internal and spiritual. A person can be very poor, yet very proud. Ultimately, pride doesn't arise from what is in our bank accounts, it arises from what is in our hearts.

With that in mind, let's look at what God's book of wisdom says about pride. It's radically different from the messages of a culture occupied with "American idols," but it's also the way to live well. We'll see that God hates pride, pride is harmful to us, and pride leads to a dreadful future.

GOD HATES PRIDE

Proverbs 16:5 says, "Everyone who is arrogant in heart is an abomination to the LORD; be assured, he will not go unpunished." Proverbs 6:17–19 lists seven things that the Lord hates. Number one on the list is "haughty eyes." That refers to a look that is exalted, or proud. So, the book of Proverbs says that pride is an abomination to God, and God hates a proud look. Why does God have such antipathy to pride? Think about what pride has done, and what it continues to do.

Pride leads to independence from God, not trust. Proverbs 3:5 is a command. It says, "Trust in the LORD with all your heart." Do we trust God in every part of our lives? Do we depend on him by faith? Pride leads us away from trust in God and toward trust in ourselves. When we're proud, we think we don't need God because we're perfectly capable of handling life on our own. The problem with that way of thinking is that God *created* us for fellowship with himself, and we'll never experience joyful life without him. Proverbs 21:4 says, "Haughty eyes and a proud heart, the lamp of the wicked, are sin."

A proud heart is sin. Our culture honors people who are independent minded and self-reliant. God's book of wisdom does not encourage us to be self-reliant; it commands us to trust in God and submit to him. Jesus even said, "Apart from me you can do nothing" (John 15:5). In light of that fact, self-reliance is a fool's errand. No wonder pride is an abomination to God. It makes fools of us, and it leads to independence from God, not trust in him.

Second, *pride leads to sin, not obedience.* The first time pride surfaced in the history of humanity, it led to sin. Before Eve ate the forbidden fruit in the garden of Eden, the serpent tempted her with pride. He said, "You will be like God" (Gen 3:5). Of course, that was a lie. Adam and Eve were already like God in that they were created in his image, and sin would cause them to be *less* like God, not more like him. But pride creates the desire to be greater and bigger, so Eve was attracted by the serpent's temptation and she ate. Eve didn't disobey God's command just for a bite of fruit. The temptation was greater than the tantalizing taste, or the appetizing appearance. She disobeyed because of a tremendous pull, a crushing pressure—the temptation of pride: "You will be like God."

Consider the devil himself. In 1 Timothy 3 the Apostle Paul lists the qualifications for overseers in the church. One of the qualifications is this: "He must not be a recent convert, or he may become puffed up with conceit and fall into the condemnation of the devil" (v. 6). Men who have not been Christians for very long are not to become overseers in the church. Why not? They may become conceited, *like the devil did.* The devil is under God's condemnation because of pride. Do you see why God hates pride so much? Pride made the devil the devil, and pride led to the first sin in the garden of Eden. Pride ushered sin into the world and ruined the human race. All the wickedness we see in our world today originated with the sin of pride. Every rape, every murder, every act of dishonesty, every kind of cruelty and perversion grew from the sin of pride. Pride is the basic sin, the sin that leads to all other sins. Pride is the sin of independence from God and rebellion against God. Pride is the attitude that we know more than God and we don't need God.

Pride is the antithesis of a right relationship with God. In the book of Proverbs, a right relationship with God is expressed by the phrase "the fear of the LORD." In Proverbs 8:13, Wisdom is speaking and she says, "The fear of the LORD is hatred of evil. Pride and arrogance and the way of evil and perverted speech I hate." When we have God's wisdom, we'll hate pride and arrogance.

PRIDE HURTS US

The book of Proverbs describes several results of pride. Once it has slithered into our hearts, it produces all kinds of wicked consequences. For example, *pride promotes personal position.* Proverbs 27:2 says, "Let another praise you, and not your own mouth; a stranger, and not your own lips." Pride causes us to praise ourselves, to seek our own glory, but God's book of wisdom tells us, "Let another praise you, and not your own mouth." When we are under the spell of pride, we don't want to wait for others to praise us. What if they forget? What if they don't praise us at the proper time when the right people can hear the praise? What if they neglect to do it altogether? That's unacceptable to pride. Proverbs 25:27 says that it is not "glorious to seek one's own glory." But seeking one's own glory is exactly what pride motivates us to do. Pride causes us to think about our glory and position.

Proverbs 25:6–7 says, "Do not put yourself forward in the king's presence or stand in the place of the great, for it is better to be told, 'Come up here,' than to be put lower in the presence of a noble." Pride makes us think, "I want to be up there with the people who are powerful and important. That's where I belong." So, we promote ourselves with prominent people in order to get ahead. God's book of wisdom tells us that is exactly what we should not do.

Luke 14:7–11 records that Jesus made the same point. He said that when we're invited to a banquet we should not take the place of honor. If we do, we may be asked to get up and go to the back, while someone more important sits in the seat of honor. Instead, Jesus said to sit in the back and we might be invited to the front. The point is that we don't promote ourselves or push ourselves to the front. We do our best to glorify God, and we let someone else promote us. Jesus concluded with these words: "For everyone who exalts himself will be humbled, and he who humbles himself will be exalted." Jesus told us to look for the last seat, but pride causes us to look for the best seat. Pride causes us to work for our advancement and to think of our image. "What do people think of me? How do I look? Do these people know who I am? Do they know what I've done?" Such thinking is the result of pride, because pride promotes personal position.

Second, *pride expresses rebellion.* Remember Proverbs 16:5? "Everyone who is arrogant in heart is an abomination to the LORD." The word "abomination" is used in the Bible for the most heinous sins a person can commit, and this verse names arrogance among them. Many people don't really think of themselves as sinners because they've never killed anybody, they don't steal, they don't cheat on their taxes, and they recycle. Great, but all of us have something in our hearts that is an abomination to God. It doesn't even have to reach the hands or the mouth to be sin. "Everyone who is arrogant *in heart* is an abomination to the LORD."

We are born with a proud, self-centered attitude in our hearts. The Bible says that we are "by nature children of wrath" (Eph 2:3). We don't have to teach children to be self-interested or selfish. We have to teach them *not* to be selfish and to be interested in the welfare of others. When a five-year-old child is happily playing a video game and another child shows up and asks for the controller so he can take a turn with the game, what happens? The first child rarely says, "Of course! How selfish of me not to offer the game to you before you had to ask for it!" No, usually the child mutters, "In a minute," and that minute drags on indefinitely until the second child finally has to beg to play. We come into the world wanting to be our own little gods, sitting on the throne with our own little joysticks, worshiping at the shrine of our own egos. That is the work of pride—it expresses our sinful rebellion.

Third, *pride produces interpersonal conflict.* Proverbs 13:10 says, "By insolence comes nothing but strife." "Insolence" translates a Hebrew word that is translated elsewhere with words like "arrogance" and "pride." Pride produces strife.

In all church strife, pride is a factor. Interpersonal dissension in the workplace also usually involves pride. All marital conflict involves pride at some point.

What if we were to do something entirely different? What if we decided that we don't want to rule over our lives anymore? What if we made Jesus the master over our lives and gave him the right to rule? What if we made Galatians 2:20 our motto? "I have been crucified with Christ. It is no longer I who live, but Christ who lives in me." If we did that, then Christ would be ruling—as the sole king—over all of our lives.

When we exalt self, the result is interpersonal conflict. When we exalt Christ, the result is harmony under his rule. That doesn't mean that we will never have any differences of opinion. If both husband and wife always think the same way, one of them isn't necessary. We will have disagreements with our spouses, but to work out the disagreements constructively, we have to eliminate pride.

The same sort of conflict happens in churches, and in all relationships. Pride asks, "How can I get my way? How can I impose my will so that I'll get everything I want?" That proud attitude leads to conflict. "By insolence comes nothing but strife." On the other hand, humility asks, "How can I serve the other person? I'm not more important than him; I'm going to make him more important than me. What can I do to help him?" Pride creates interpersonal conflict, but humility creates interpersonal harmony.

Fourth, *pride creates false security*. Proverbs 30:12 refers to a particular kind of person: "There are those who are clean in their own eyes but are not washed of their filth." That verse describes someone who is dirty but thinks he is clean. Such delusion is the essence of pride. A lot of people who reject the gospel of Christ and his lordship think this way: "I'm as good as the next person. Repent of sin? Ask God for forgiveness? Need the new birth? I take care of my family, I'm a respectable neighbor, and I even attend church." People who think that way are "clean in their own eyes but are not washed of their filth." Pride creates false spiritual security.

Pride convinces us that we are better than we really are. It blinds us to our weaknesses. A proud lion asked a zebra, "Who is the greatest animal in the forest?" The zebra answered, "You are the greatest, O mighty lion." The lion then asked a monkey, "Who is the greatest animal in the forest?" The monkey said, "You are the greatest, O mighty lion." Next, the lion asked an elephant, "Who is the greatest animal in the forest?" The elephant picked up the lion with his trunk and slammed him to the ground several times, and the lion said, "Well, just because you don't know the answer doesn't mean you have to get mad about it." Pride deludes us into thinking that we're greater than we really are, even when there is abundant evidence that we are not as great as we think we are.

Jesus told a parable about a man who was inflated spiritually. Luke 18 records that Jesus described a Pharisee who went to the temple to pray. The man stood and prayed, "God, I thank you that I am not like other men, extortioners, unjust, adulterers. ... I fast twice a week; I give tithes of all that I get" (vv. 11–12). His pride caused him to boast about his goodness. He was so proud that he even looked down on someone else who was also in the temple praying. He said, "I thank you that I am not like ... this tax collector." The tax collector was praying too, but it was a different kind of prayer. Jesus said that he was standing far off, unwilling to even lift up his eyes to heaven, and he prayed, "God, be merciful to me, a sinner."

What was the outcome of the prayers of those two men? Jesus concluded his parable with these words: "I tell you, this man went down to his house justified, rather than the other. For everyone who exalts himself will be humbled, but the one who humbles himself will be exalted" (Luke 18:14). The Pharisee went home from the temple dignified in his own eyes and the eyes of society. The tax collector went home justified, forgiven and reconciled to God.

A proud heart will listen to the devil when he whispers, "Keep your dignity; don't admit that you need forgiveness. You don't need God to free you and cleanse you. Cleanse you from what?" Pride blinds people to their need for forgiveness and reconciliation with God. But when we see God's holiness and our sin, we can see that a sacrifice for sin was necessary and that Christ was the one who offered himself as the sacrifice. When we look at the cross and realize that the sacrificial death of Jesus was necessary because of the sin in our hearts, then pride melts away. The hymn writer Isaac Watts understood that. He wrote,

> When I survey the wondrous cross,
> On which the Prince of Glory died;
> My richest gain I count but loss,
> And pour contempt on all my pride.[3]

Pride creates false security in our own goodness. The truth is that no one is so good that he doesn't need to be saved, and no one is so bad that Jesus cannot save him.

PRIDE LEADS TO A DREADFUL FUTURE

What does the future hold for those who are proud? It's not pretty. Pride's outcome is pretty scary because so many people are controlled by pride but are blind to it. Therefore, many people will face pride's future but are totally unprepared for it.

The book of Proverbs specifies at least two future outcomes for pride. First is *humiliation*. Isn't that ironic? The proud person is looking for exaltation and honor, but pride leads only to humiliation. Proverbs 11:2 says, "When pride comes, then comes disgrace." Proverbs 29:23 says, "One's pride will bring him low, but he who is lowly in spirit will obtain honor." Pride brings us down; humility leads to honor.

God has laid down a rule in life—the way up is down. In Matthew 23:11-12, Jesus said, "The greatest among you shall be your servant. Whoever exalts himself will be humbled, and whoever humbles himself will be exalted." The devil was proud, but he was brought low. Jesus humbled himself and became a servant, so Philippians 2:9 says, "Therefore God has highly exalted him and bestowed on him the name that is above every name." Which lifestyle will we follow? Jesus' way of humble service seems to be down, but it's up. The devil's way of pride seems to be up, but it's down.

Second, pride leads to *destruction*. Proverbs 15:25 says, "The LORD tears down the house of the proud." Proverbs 16:18 says, "Pride goes before destruction, and a haughty spirit before a fall." Proverbs 18:12 says, "Before destruction a man's heart is haughty." Pride leads to the destruction of homes as husbands and wives fight one another instead of fighting their problems. Pride leads to the destruction of relationships as people insist on getting their own way instead of serving one another. Pride leads to financial destruction as people try to keep up with the Joneses. Pride leads to emotional destruction as we worry what other people think of us.

Worst of all, pride brings spiritual and eternal destruction. People who are outside of Christ are not merely going to be humiliated; they're going to be condemned forever. Many people who will spend eternity in hell will be there because they were proud. They thought they had no need for God, no need for a Savior from sin. But when we heed God's book of wisdom we will live well now and forever. In Proverbs God stresses that humility is necessary. He repeatedly exhorts us to listen to instruction, to learn wisdom, and to follow wisdom's ways. Pride works against that because it deludes us into thinking that we already know everything.

Follow a different way—the way of God's wisdom—and acknowledge that God hates pride, recognize that pride expresses our depraved nature, and realize that pride leads to humiliation and destruction. It's sad but true—all of us are infected with the disease of pride. God has the cure. Apply it and live well.

QUESTIONS FOR
REFLECTION

1. Do you think you have a clear understanding of your weaknesses and failures, or does pride sometimes blind you to your faults?

2. How often has pride caused you to rely on yourself rather than trust in God? When that happens, how should you respond? What can prevent such self-reliance in the future?

3. How have you seen pride result in interpersonal conflict? What attitudes and/or actions would have prevented the conflict?

4. Why is pride especially inappropriate for followers of Jesus?

CHAPTER 7

HOLINESS, HAPPINESS, AND HEALTH

The Bible affirms that a holy relationship with God gives us joy, and that joy contributes to our health. Occasionally I read reports that emphasize the truths underscored in this chapter. For example, professors Andrew Clark and Orsolya Lelkes wrote about their research on the effectiveness of religion in buffering the impact that stressful events have on a person's wellbeing. They showed that people who are religious enjoy higher levels of life satisfaction and that religion insures against some adverse life events. They wrote, "All denominations suffer less psychological harm from unemployment than do the non-religious." The same is true with respect to marital difficulties.[1]

Medical experts Robert Ornstein and David Sobel presented the results of their research in their book *Healthy Pleasures*. Their thesis is that happiness is the most important ingredient in a healthy life. They wrote,

> We discovered that the most hardy people we know do not follow all the "correct" advice about health. Their health secrets don't lie in the proscriptions and prescriptions that leap from almost every magazine and television program. Some assault the government's dietary guidelines at nearly every meal. ... The positive moods and pleasurable expectations of healthy people were so striking to us. ... As a rule, they were optimistic and happy.[2]

Harold G. Koenig has devoted years to researching the relationship between the condition of our spirits and the condition of our bodies. In a 2008 book entitled *Medicine, Religion, and Health,* he wrote,

> It appears that psychological and social factors influence the physiological systems of the body that are directly responsible for good health and the ability to fight disease. ... Religious factors may improve physical health as well, doing so by reducing psychological stress, increasing social support, and encouraging positive health behaviors.[3]

Studies like these address the relationship between the condition of our minds and emotions on the one hand, and the condition of our bodies on the other. The fact that they are all dynamically related is now being broadly acknowledged in Western culture. A magazine is published called *Spirituality and Health.* An academic society exists that is called the Society for Spirituality, Theology, and Health. They publish a journal called *Crossroads,* and at their annual meeting, papers are presented that explore and demonstrate the interconnection between spiritual health and physical health. When a new study is released to the public, the media often portrays the results as groundbreaking, astonishing. However, such studies are actually repeating a reality that has long been expressed more fully in God's book of wisdom.

Both medical science and the Bible show that a connection exists between happiness and health. The Bible goes further. It states that a connection also exists between holiness and happiness. Holiness leads to happiness, and happiness contributes to health. Therefore, if we want to be healthy we should be happy, and if we want to be happy we should be holy. Consider the wisdom of Proverbs 14:30: "A tranquil heart gives life to the flesh, but envy makes the bones rot." Proverbs 17:22 says, "A joyful heart is good medicine, but a crushed spirit dries up the bones." This is another way God's book of wisdom helps us to live well: it shows us the dynamic connection between sadness and sickness, between happiness and health, and it teaches us how to find happiness.

A CRUSHED SPIRIT BURDENS US

Proverbs 12:25 says, "Anxiety in a man's heart weighs him down." Everyone experiences anxiety, fear, or worry. A friend told me that she was on her way to speak at a women's conference on the subject of fear, anxiety, and worry. She said that she was really fearful, anxious, and worried about it! It's not difficult to *understand* how to conquer anxiety. The challenge is actually *doing* it. The Bible says that anxiety weighs us down. Anxiety is a weight, a burden. The second part of Proverbs 17:22 says, "A crushed spirit dries up the bones." When our spirits are broken, or burdened with anxiety, our health is affected negatively. Also, consider Proverbs 15:13: "A glad heart makes a cheerful face, but by sorrow of heart the spirit is crushed."

Have you ever seen someone with a crushed spirit? Maybe you have had a crushed spirit, or maybe you feel that your spirit is crushed right now. When someone has a crushed spirit, the joy of living fades, enthusiasm dies. A crushed spirit has physical consequences too. Sometimes the physical consequences are immediate, and sometimes they are eventual. Samuel Ullman wrote:

> Youth is not a time of life. It is a state of mind. It is not a matter of red cheeks ... and supple knees. It is a temper of the will, ... a vigor of the emotions. ... This often exists in a man of fifty, more than in a boy of twenty. Nobody grows old by merely living a number of years. ... Years may wrinkle the skin, but to give up enthusiasm wrinkles the soul. Worry, doubt ... fear and despair, these are the long, long years that bow the head. ... You are as young as your faith, as old as your doubt; as young as your self-confidence, as old as your fear; as young as your hope, as old as your despair.[4]

Ullman had observed what the Bible says: "A crushed spirit dries up the bones." The condition of our spirits affects our bodies, and when the spirit is broken, our health falters and withers. Doctors refer to "emotionally induced illnesses" and "psychosomatic conditions." The condition of our emotions and the condition of our bodies are dynamically related. "A crushed spirit dries up the bones." "Anxiety in a man's heart weighs him down."

So, how can we remove the burden of a crushed spirit? Is there some leverage we can use to lift the weight that crushes us? Obviously, living well does not include anxiety and a crushed spirit. So yes, God's book of wisdom helps us remove such things and enjoy the good life.

A JOYFUL SPIRIT BENEFITS US

The book of Proverbs says that a broken spirit has a negative effect on our health. The opposite is also true. A joyful spirit has a positive effect on our physical condition. Proverbs 14:30 says, "A tranquil heart gives life to the flesh." Proverbs 15:15

says, "All the days of the afflicted are evil, but the cheerful of heart has a continual feast." What a statement! "The cheerful of heart has a continual feast." Of course, Proverbs is not addressing realities like chemical imbalances that lead to depression and anxiety. Such imbalances are the result of the universal effects of the fall of humanity into sin. Everyone's body is affected by sin, and as a result some people struggle with imbalances that have profound emotional consequences that require specialized care to address. People who have been changed by God's grace and who live according to his wisdom will show compassion to those who struggle with such problems and will help provide the needed care.

Living wisely is also a kind of specialized care. The first part of Proverbs 17:22 says, "A joyful heart is good medicine." The Hebrew word translated "medicine" refers to a healing or cure, something that sets us free from bodily affliction. So, to return to Proverbs 17:22, "A joyful heart is a good healing, a cure." Early in this chapter we cited a few studies that indicate that medical science is affirming that the condition of the psyche is related to the ability of the body to resist disease and infection. Long ago, God said that a joyful heart frees us from that which threatens our health.[5]

Nehemiah 8:10 says, "The joy of the LORD is your strength." Joy is strong medicine, and the joy of the Lord is extra-strength medicine. Walking in fellowship with the Lord and separating ourselves from sin gives us a clear conscience. With a clear conscience, we sleep better at night so that our bodies get plenty of rest. When we trust in the Lord we aren't full of anxiety, so our bodies digest food better. We don't eat compulsively because the source of our peace and comfort is not food but the Lord. We don't do things that are harmful to the body because we know it's the temple of the Holy Spirit. So, Nehemiah 8:10 literally comes to pass in our lives: "The joy of the LORD is your strength."

Our joy and our health are dynamically related. Further, our joy is linked inseparably with the health of our relationship with God. Joy leads to good health, and joy results from holiness. Our happiness is a spiritual matter in several ways.

First, *joy reveals the condition of our spirits.* Joy is a barometer of our spiritual condition. When Paul wrote his letter to the Philippians, he was in jail and facing the possibility of execution in the near future. In the midst of that gloomy situation, Paul wrote that some good things had resulted from his imprisonment: Roman guards had heard the gospel from him, and other Christians had seen Paul's example and had become bolder in their witness. So, in Philippians 1:18 Paul writes, "In that I rejoice. Yes, and I will rejoice."

Because of Paul's relationship with Christ, he realized that the proclamation of the gospel was more important than his comfort, even more important than his life. Therefore, Paul was able to be happy in the midst of adverse circumstances. He refused to derive his joy from the status of his creature comforts. Instead, he derived his joy from the Lord. When our spiritual condition is right, we'll do the same. And we'll know that we're deriving our joy from the Lord when we have joy in the midst of suffering, as did Paul. Our joy is a gauge, a barometer, of our spiritual condition.

Second, *joy is inherent to our salvation.* In Peter's first letter to the Christians in Asia Minor, he considered our salvation in Christ, and he broke into a hymn of praise to the Lord. He wrote,

> Blessed be the God and Father of our Lord Jesus Christ! According to his great mercy, he has caused us to be born again to a living hope through the resurrection of Jesus Christ from the dead, to an inheritance that is imperishable, undefiled, and unfading, kept in heaven for you, who by God's power are being guarded. (1 Pet 1:3–5)

What a wonderful description of salvation in Christ! Then, Peter wrote, "In this you rejoice" (v. 6). In what do we rejoice? We rejoice that we have been born again and we have a living hope kept in heaven for us. But notice what Peter wrote next. The Christians to whom Peter was writing were facing opposition and undergoing persecution, so Peter wrote, "In this you rejoice, though now for a little while, if necessary, you have been grieved by various trials" (v. 6). We're going to face some trials, and we will be "grieved" by them. But even when we experience terrible difficulties, we will still have something to be happy about. "In this you rejoice." No matter what happens, we still have new life in Christ, we're alive on the inside and will live forever, and our eternal life is imperishable and protected by the power of God.

Every person reading this chapter has had problems and will have problems. Someone has said that everyone is either in a storm, coming out of a storm, or about to go through a storm. But if you don't have anything to be happy about, you must not know Christ. People who have Christ's salvation always have *this* to be happy about—we were separated from God and carrying the burden of sin, but Christ reconciled us to God and separated our sin from us as far as the east is from the west. In that we rejoice.

A third reason our joy is important is that *joy affects our service.* One of the greatest testimonies we have is the joy of the Lord. That's how our witness for Christ becomes winsome. A cold, dry faith has no appeal to people. Many people have been turned off to Christ because some of the people who claim to be his followers are such sourpusses. I once received an advertisement for a spiritual renewal conference. It was a brochure inviting people to attend the conference, and pictures of the main speakers were on the cover of the brochure. One of the speakers looked so unhappy, so dour and disconsolate, that I said, "Why should I go to listen to *that* person talk about spiritual renewal? If looking like that is the result, why would anybody want anything to do with what they're talking about?" Christians who do not have the joy of the Lord are not very good advertisements for the life we have in Christ. People can see they are not very happy.

I once read about some gold prospectors out west who discovered a rich mine. They said, "We'll get rich from this mine as long as we don't tell anybody about what we found before we stake our claims." So, they made a vow of secrecy, but they had to go into town for supplies. When they left the town, a crowd of people followed them. The people knew they had found something because the happiness was written all over their faces. Jesus is infinitely more valuable than gold. He is the pearl of great price. When we find him, the natural result is joy that cannot be contained, and others will see in our lives the joy that Jesus brings.

START BUILDING A JOYFUL SPIRIT

Joy is important and valuable, so everyone wants more joy. Everyone is looking for happiness. Where do we find it? People look for joy in material things, in human relationships, in exotic experiences. We'll conclude this chapter by looking at some New Testament verses that express some practical ways we develop joy.

First, *our joy is important to God.* God is not only concerned about our happiness, he actually commands us to be joyful. Philippians 4:4 is an imperative: "Rejoice in the Lord always; again I will say, rejoice." We should not be surprised that God commands our joy—since our joy is a barometer of our spiritual condition, it is inherent in our salvation, and it affects our witness for him. God says, "Rejoice in the Lord always." Our joy is important to God.

Second, *joy comes from knowing Jesus.* Are you sure that you have received Jesus as your Savior? If not, do it now. Put your faith in him and ask him to come into your life. Then, you will have access to the joy that can be found only in him. The world, the flesh, and the devil conspire to convince people that sin brings more fun and happiness than Jesus. When people hear about Jesus and his salvation, the Holy Spirit begins to show them their need for Jesus. But then the devil whispers in their ears, "If you follow Jesus, you'll lose all your friends and you'll leave all your fun. You'll become a religious nut. The only music you'll listen to is organ music, and the only time you'll watch TV is when movies like *The Ten Commandments* are on." It takes the devil about thirty seconds to turn Christian discipleship into a freak show in the minds of people who are considering Christ.

That is the devil's lie. Psalm 84:11 tells the truth. It says, "The LORD God is a sun and shield. ... No good thing does he withhold from those who walk uprightly." God does not withhold anything good from us; he withholds only the things that will hurt us. Jesus said, "I came that they may have life and have it abundantly" (John 10:10). In other words, Jesus said, "Hey, all you people who think that following me is going to be a bore—you should know that the reason I came was *so that* you can have abundant life." Jesus also said this: "These things I have spoken to you, that my joy may be in you, and that your joy may be full" (John 15:11). Jesus said that if we want joy, then we should follow him. He wants to give us his joy. To have Jesus in our hearts is to have joy, and that joy is strong medicine. We could even say that if joy is not in our hearts Jesus is not in charge, because Jesus brings joy. A lot of people are not happy even though they're involved in the church; their fellowship with Jesus has grown cold or infrequent.

Third, *God can carry our burdens*. We all have burdens sometimes, and some burdens are very heavy. Even when we're following Jesus faithfully we will experience problems. But one key to joy is obeying God's command to let him carry our burdens. He can carry our burdens, and he can also carry us. First Peter 5:7 says, "Casting all your anxieties on him, because he cares for you." Psalm 55:22 says, "Cast your burden on the LORD, and he will sustain you." What burden are you carrying? What is draining your joy? "Cast your burden upon the LORD, and he will sustain you." Give your burden to the Lord.

A man was walking down a road on a hot day. He was burdened by a heavy sack of grain that he was carrying on his shoulders. Another man went by in a wagon pulled by a horse. The man in the wagon stopped his horses and said to the man who was walking with the burden, "It's too hot for you to be walking and carrying that heavy load. Climb up here in the wagon, and I'll give you a ride." The man with the load of grain on his shoulders climbed into the wagon and sat down. After a while, the man driving the wagon looked behind him at his passenger, and he saw that the man still had the sack of grain on his shoulders. He told him, "Please, put down that grain and relax!" But the man said, "Oh, no. You're already giving *me* a ride; I couldn't ask you to carry my load too." Like that man in the wagon, we sometimes forget that our God is well capable of carrying our burdens. If we let him carry us, he carries our burdens too. He wants to carry us and our burdens because he loves us.

True joy is found in Christ, and that joy is God's medicine. If you want to be healthy, you should be happy, and if you want to be happy, you'll find joy in Christ.

QUESTIONS FOR REFLECTION

1. How does the joy of the Lord become our strength? Do you typically experience the joy of the Lord each day?
2. What can followers of Jesus be happy about in every circumstance?

3. When you have a burden, is your first impulse to grit your teeth and bear the burden yourself, or to give the burden to God? Have you given all your burdens to God? If not, why not do it right now and enjoy living well!

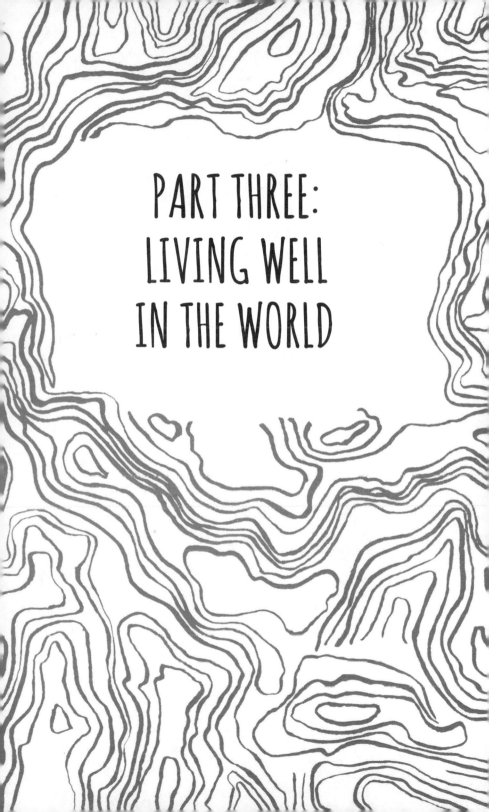

PART THREE:
LIVING WELL
IN THE WORLD

CHAPTER 8

DOLLARS AND SENSE

MOST PEOPLE DON'T HANDLE MONEY VERY WELL. THE financial crisis of 2008 screamed that message. Mortgages collapsed because people took on too much debt so they could live in larger houses than they could afford. Banks folded because they took on too much risk by extending loans to people whose ability to repay was questionable (leading one man to quip, "My checks cleared, but my bank bounced"). Even large companies overestimated the stability of the market and overextended themselves into bankruptcy. In the midst of the crisis, the new secretary of the treasury admitted that he had not paid his own taxes correctly, and Congress approved the distribution of enormous amounts of money with no guarantee that spending taxpayer monies would actually improve the economy. Most people don't handle money very well.

Also, most people want more money than they have. Americans live in the most prosperous nation in the world, but no one seems to have as much money as they want. An unprecedented number of families have two incomes, yet family consumer debt climbs higher and higher. We seem to be living by the motto, "Live within your income, even if you have to borrow to do it." Counselors say that one of the most common causes of family contention and divorce is conflict over money. All of this is not because we have less money than former generations. It's because we want more. The Bible warns us about loving money. First Timothy 6:10 says, "The love of money is a root of all kinds of evils. It is through this craving that some have wandered away from the faith and pierced themselves with many pangs." The way we relate to money can cause all sorts of problems. On the other hand, when we learn and live God's principles of wisdom concerning possessions, we will be blessed.

None of us has unlimited resources, and most of us have had what has been called an out-of-money experience. A lot of people ask why they don't have more money. They thought that when they got that raise or landed a better job things would be better, but things don't seem any better. Other people wonder why they haven't received that raise or why they haven't been able to find a job that would provide a better income. One fellow said that he had heard that money talks, "But," he said, "All mine says is good-bye."

Many verses in Proverbs address the subject of finances. God's wisdom on wealth is immediately applicable and as current as tomorrow's stock market report. Maybe you have a broker or financial advisor. While reading this chapter, allow God to be your financial advisor and consider what he says to you about handling wealth wisely. I have summarized the wisdom of Proverbs on this subject under five headings, and I express them as imperatives.

WORK HARD

Proverbs 6:10-11 says, "A little sleep, a little slumber, a little folding of the hands to rest, and poverty will come upon you like a robber, and want like an armed man." Proverbs 20:13 says, "Love not sleep, lest you come to poverty; open your eyes, and you will have plenty of bread." In other words, if you want your needs to be met, wake up, get out of bed, and go to work. My wife and I had a conversation with a young lady who had recently graduated from college and was in her first full-time job. She said she liked adult life, but the problem was that it starts too early in the morning. Most of us can relate to that sentiment, but God's book of wisdom commends getting up and working for our income. When we do that, our needs will be met.

Some people take rather extreme measures to avoid working for their income. A mafia boss hired a deaf bookkeeper, thinking that since the bookkeeper wouldn't hear anything, he couldn't testify to anything in court. But the mafia boss learned that the bookkeeper cheated him out of $10 million. The mafia boss paid the bookkeeper a visit, and he took an assistant with him who knew sign language. When they arrived, the boss told his assistant, "Ask him where he put the $10 million." The assistant signed the question to the deaf bookkeeper. The bookkeeper signed back, "I have no idea what he's talking about." When the assistant told the mafia boss what the bookkeeper had said, the mafia boss pulled out a handgun, held it to the bookkeeper's head, and said, "Ask him again where he put the $10 million." The assistant signed to the bookkeeper, "He'll kill you if you don't tell him!" And the bookkeeper signed back, "Ok, you win. It's in a brown briefcase buried by the shed in my cousin's backyard." The mafia boss asked his assistant, "What did he say?" The assistant told him, "He said that you don't have the guts to pull the trigger." People will do almost anything for money. The Bible affirms that if we want more money, we ought to work toward an increase in industry. Our work is such a major subject in Proverbs, and a major factor in living well, that we'll address it more fully in the next chapter.

DON'T BE
IMPETUOUS

A lot of people are impetuous, or impatient, with money. Proverbs 21:5 says, "The plans of the diligent lead surely to abundance, but everyone who is hasty comes only to poverty." According to that verse, who has abundance? It's the diligent person who plans. Being "hasty" to get wealth, however, leads to poverty. Some people are in a hurry to gain wealth. As a result, they're impetuous with wealth, making decisions based on impatience, and that rarely leads to profit. Proverbs 28:20 says, "A faithful man will abound with blessings, but whoever hastens to be rich will not go unpunished."

What does it mean to be hasty with our finances, or to hasten to be rich? It may mean buying into a get-rich-quick scheme. Usually, people who are impatient to be rich and buy into a get-rich-quick scheme wind up wasting their income and energies. They start out to become a millionaire by age forty, but they wind up putting huge amounts of stress on their budgets, their health, their spiritual condition, and their families. That's one reason gambling is a bad idea. It's an attempt to gain wealth without work (Prov 6:10–11; 20:13; 1 Thess 5:14; 2 Thess 3:10–12); it's driven by impatience to be wealthy, which is inevitably materialistic (Prov 28:20; 1 Tim 6:6–11); since a lot of people are addicted to gambling, it capitalizes on the misery of other people instead of helping them (Acts 20:33–35; 1 Thess 5:14); and gambling is ultimately idolatry, because it is trusting in chance to provide for our needs rather than trusting in God (Ps 37:3–5; Col 3:5; 1 Tim 6:17–19).

Gambling is not the only way we can be hasty to be rich. Years ago, I had a friend who was in a business related to the oil industry. He amassed a significant amount of wealth in a short span of time. As a young man, he paid cash for his house, his Mercedes, his speedboat, his Jet Skis—you get the picture. Then, a criminal investigation was conducted into the activities of the company for which he worked. The company was found guilty of fraud, and so was my friend. He said that he had not known that what he was doing was illegal, but he was sentenced to federal prison, and his friends were left to wonder, "Shouldn't he have known that making that much money that quickly sounded too good to be true, and if it sounds too good to be true it probably is?" The lure of wealth is so powerful, it will make people do things that they would not otherwise do, and it will blind people to things they would otherwise have seen. The lure of wealth is especially powerful to those who are hasty to be rich.

DON'T INDULGE
IN VANITY

Proverbs 28:19 says, "Whoever works his land will have plenty of bread, but he who follows worthless pursuits will have plenty of poverty." "Worthless" can also be translated "vain" or "empty." Those who pursue empty, worthless things will experience hardship. Proverbs 12:11 says, "Whoever works his land will have plenty of bread, but he who follows worthless pursuits lacks sense." What are some pursuits that are vain, or worthless? Usually, we can find some of those in our entertainment budgets. Some people say that they can't afford to give generously to the work of God's kingdom in the world, but somehow they can afford to purchase a boat, a sports car, and a Caribbean vacation. That scenario has been repeated so many times that it has actually affected the entire economy: people buy a larger house than their budget can support, they borrow excessively in order to do it, and they default on the loan. Or, they buy a $40,000 car when they could have spent $20,000. Why do they do that? "I have always wanted that kind of car." That's a vain pursuit.

Even a healthy hobby can become a vain pursuit if it dominates too much of our thinking, our time, or our pocketbooks.

It's also possible to be vain by spending money on expensive clothes with the most fashionable labels. Some people want to be seen only in clothes that have the right emblem on them. That's vanity, and it's being a poor steward of the resources God allows us to have. Certainly it's possible to become legalistic about how much money people spend on clothes, cars, etc., and becoming judgmental about such things is not right since the Bible has no command concerning our discretionary budget. However, it is appropriate and helpful for all of us to examine our hearts about how we spend the money God allows us to have. Does any of our spending suggest vanity?

On the other hand, God has given commands about some vain pursuits. The Bible describes them as sinful, and one consequence of such sin is stress on the family budget. A young couple came to me for counseling, and one of their problems was finances. As we talked the husband stated that he went to bars occasionally, and it wasn't unusual for him to spend over $150 in one night in a bar. For some reason, it had not occurred to him that there could be a connection between his vain pursuit and their financial pressure. I wanted to say to him what my father used to say to me: "Use your head for something besides a hat rack." That's why this chapter is entitled "Dollars and Sense." God wants us to be wise with our finances, so he has given us wise counsel in his word to help us avoid foolish mistakes.

Proverbs 23:21 says, "The drunkard and the glutton will come to poverty, and slumber will clothe them with rags." Heavy drinking and gluttony lead to poverty, and heavy drinking and gluttony are indulging in vain pursuits. It's likely that almost everyone reading this book knows a family that has suffered financially because somebody in that family has spent money to support an alcohol habit. All of us have also seen alcoholics on the street with only the second-hand clothes on their backs. They are literally clothed "with rags." It's even possible to spend an unnecessary amount of money on food. Some families put financial pressure on themselves by eating out when they can't afford it, or buying lots of snack foods and constantly eating them, or just eating too much in general. Heavy drinking and gluttony are alike in that they abuse and waste the resources God provides for us. The situation is compounded by the reality that gluttons and heavy drinkers have more difficulty finding a job that pays adequately and keeping that job. Sinful indulgence can cause financial hardship.

Beyond the matter of debits and credits on an accounting ledger, spiritual realities are at work here. Even when people have large incomes, they invite problems when they indulge in vain pursuits. On the other hand, even when people have small incomes, they will have enough when they live and spend wisely. God promised as much to the poor but generous Macedonian Christians: "God is able to make all grace abound to you, so that having all sufficiency in all things at all times, you may abound in every good work" (2 Cor 9:8). When we are sowing seed in the right places, God supplies seed to the sower. When we are doing God's will, he supplies us with the resources so that we "may abound in every good work."

PURSUE GENEROSITY

God's people are to be generous. The Bible affirms that unambiguously and repeatedly. The book of Proverbs expresses that truth with lucid imagery. Proverbs 11:24-25 says, "One gives freely, yet grows all the richer; another withholds what he should give, and only suffers want. Whoever brings blessing will be enriched, and one who waters will himself be watered." That's an amazing principle, and it's one of the keys to enjoying a happy life. The person who scatters, giving away his resources, increases all the more. The person who withholds, or is stingy, does not enjoy blessing. The person who waters others will be watered; God will meet the needs of that person.

These verses express a spiritual principle that is common throughout the Bible. Some have called this principle the law of the harvest. The law of the harvest is that God blesses his people when they give. In 2 Corinthians 9:6, Paul puts it this way: "Whoever sows sparingly will also reap sparingly, and whoever sows bountifully will also reap bountifully." God blesses his people when they give, and he blesses them in proportion to their gift. This principle is not the same as the "health and wealth" gospel, and Paul wasn't a prosperity preacher. He was anything but that. Paul suffered for the sake of the gospel, and he promised that others who are faithful to the gospel will suffer too. Still, under the inspiration of the Holy Spirit he wrote that when we generously invest our lives and resources in God's work in the world, God will meet our needs. When we are sowing his seeds, he will supply seed to the sower, and the more we sow the more he supplies. No health and wealth gospel is in that truth, only a promise that when we are generous in kingdom giving God will graciously meet our needs.

In practical terms, how does this work? Suppose a family is making $75,000 a year and is making just enough money to pay the bills. Then they begin giving ten percent or more to God's work, so they only have about $65,000 a year. Yet, they still have enough. How does that work? It usually *doesn't* work in isolation from the other principles the Bible teaches about money. In other words, at the same time we prioritize obedience to God in giving, our spending on vain things diminishes. It has always worked for my family and for many others. We really don't have to know how it works. We only have to obey God and trust him to be true to his word. Many Christians say they trust God, but they don't trust him with their checkbooks, so they don't really trust him. They're deceiving themselves. "One gives freely, yet grows all the richer; another withholds what he should give, and only suffers want. Whoever brings blessing will be enriched, and one who waters will himself be watered" (Prov 11:24–25).

The book of Proverbs also describes the benefits that accrue to those who give generously. First, when we give generously, *God will be honored*. God is glorified by the generosity of his people. Proverbs 14:31 says, "Whoever oppresses a poor man insults his Maker, but he who is generous to the needy honors him." When we give, we honor God because we are being obedient to him. When we give to needy people we're honoring God because our gift is a statement that needy people are worthy of help; they are created and loved by God. The fact that they are not powerful or wealthy and cannot do anything for us doesn't mean that they're insignificant or small. God made them, so they're valuable. "Whoever oppresses a poor man insults his Maker, but he who is generous to the needy honors him."

Second, when we give generously *we will be blessed*, or happy. Proverbs 14:21 says, "Blessed is he who is generous to the poor." Jesus also connected our giving and our happiness. He said, "It is more blessed to give than to receive" (Acts 20:35). This is one of the reasons the devil has so commonly attacked people in the church in the area of giving. He has tempted us to have resistance and even resentment concerning generous giving. Why? First of all, the giving of God's people funds evangelism and missions, and the devil doesn't want anyone to hear the truth about Jesus. Second, the devil knows that the result of giving will be the joy of God's people, so he attempts to keep Christians emotionally poor by convincing us that it's more blessed to receive than to give. But God says, "Blessed is he who is generous to the poor."

A third and similar benefit of generosity is that *we will be prosperous*. Proverbs 3:9 is a command: "Honor the LORD with your wealth and with the firstfruits of all your produce." Giving honors God, and God's people are commanded to honor him in that way. The second part of verse 9 says that we're to honor him by giving him the first—not the last, not even the second. "Honor the Lord ... with the *firstfruits* of all your produce." We don't determine what we give to God in worship by looking at our checking account balance on Sunday morning and saying, "Let's see what we have left to give to God. Hmm. We don't have enough to give much this week. Maybe we can give something next week." Instead, we are to honor the Lord by giving to him first. When we are paid, the first check we write is the one to the Lord through his church—"the firstfruits of all your produce." For our family that has always meant giving at least a tithe *before* taxes are taken out of our income, not after taxes. When we give after taxes, the government gets the first, and we give to God out of what's left over after the government is paid.

After the command of Proverbs 3:9 comes the promise: "Then your barns will be filled with plenty, and your vats will be bursting with wine." Full barns and overflowing vats are pictures of prosperity. Honoring God by giving him the first leads to prosperity. God blesses his people when they give. That doesn't mean that we give in order to get. Don't buy into the distortions of health and wealth preachers and conclude, "I want to be prosperous, so I'll give $1,000 so I can get $2,000 from God." That is giving with the motive of covetousness, hoping to gain by a so-called generous act. In 1 Timothy 6:5, Paul wrote about people who give "imagining that godliness is a means of gain." He called them "depraved in mind and deprived of the truth." "Depraved" and "deprived"—that's quite an unflattering description of people who give to get.

In contrast with that sort of thinking, the Bible says that we're to give generously to honor and obey God. Then, because God is gracious, he will insure that we are not deprived of any

good thing. He will bless us with his joy and care for us by giving us enough. The Bible affirms that repeatedly. For example, Proverbs 28:27 says, "Whoever gives to the poor will not
want." Proverbs 22:9 says, "Whoever has a bountiful eye will
be blessed, for he shares his bread with the poor." When we
give, we will be blessed.

Fourth, when we are generous, *we will have greater influence.* Generous people are respected, and other people want
to be their friends. Proverbs 18:16 says, "A man's gift makes
room for him and brings him before the great." Someone
who gives has an entrée into the presence of other big-
hearted, generous people. Proverbs 19:6 says, "Many seek the
favor of a generous man, and everyone is a friend to a man
who gives gifts." Who is more likely to have a lot of friends—
the person who buys a birthday gift for as little as he can possibly spend, or the person who gives extravagantly, lavish-
ing love on others? "Everyone is a friend to a man who gives
gifts." Generous people are usually happy people, and everybody wants to be around happy people, not people who are
stingy or selfish.

Suppose someone is angry with you. Proverbs 21:14 says,
"A gift in secret averts anger." A gift averts anger. Generosity
actually helps us to have happy and healthy relationships
with other people. People who give to others, even to people
with whom they have conflict, subdue anger. That helps us to
be peacemakers, and Jesus said, "Blessed are the peacemakers,
for they shall be called sons of God" (Matt 5:9). Giving a gift
makes peace with people. If you're in conflict with someone,
it's amazing how a gift of brownies contributes to resolving
that conflict. If you ever have conflict with me, some icing on
the brownies would help even more. When we give, it helps us
to build relationships of friendship, love, and respect. Those
relationships help us to be successful in every way, and our
influence will be extended.

I have saved the best benefit of giving for last: *We will have eternal rewards*. We have seen that God blesses us in *this* life when we give generously, but Proverbs 19:17 says, "Whoever is generous to the poor lends to the LORD, and he will repay him for his deed." What a marvelous, miraculous truth. When we give to someone in need, we're also giving to the Lord. But the Lord says that it's not really a gift to him; it's a loan, because he's going to pay us back for our gift to the poor. "Whoever is generous to the poor *lends* to the LORD, and he will repay him for his deed."

In the Gospel of Matthew Jesus speaks of a scene at the end of the age, when he will come with the angels in all his glory. All the nations will be gathered before him, and he will separate all people into those who are his and those who are not his. He will say to those who are his,

> Come, you who are blessed by my Father, inherit the kingdom prepared for you from the foundation of the world. For I was hungry and you gave me food, I was thirsty and you gave me drink, I was a stranger and you welcomed me, I was naked and you clothed me, I was sick and you visited me, I was in prison and you came to me. (Matt 25:34–36)

Jesus said that the righteous will say, "Lord, when did we do all of that for you? When did we feed you, or give you something to drink, or clothe you, or visit you?" Jesus said that he'll answer that by saying, "Truly, I say to you, as you did it to one of the least of these my brothers, you did it to me" (Matt 25:40). What did Proverbs 19:17 say? "Whoever is generous to the poor lends to *the* LORD, and he will repay him for his deed." Likewise, Jesus said that when we give to "the least of these," we give to *him*, and we will receive eternal rewards.

Jesus also said, "Do not lay up for yourselves treasures on earth, where moth and rust destroy and where thieves break in and steal, but lay up for yourselves treasures in heaven, where neither moth nor rust destroys and where thieves do not break in and steal" (Matt 6:19-20). We can store up treasures in heaven. Sometimes when a baby is born, the proud parents will open a savings account for that child. Periodically, they will deposit money into the account, saving it for the day when it will be given to the child. The child of God has a spiritual account in heaven. Jesus said, "Lay up for yourselves treasures in heaven." Where are you storing up treasures— on earth or in heaven? Thank God that a benefit of generosity is eternal reward.

REJECT WRONG PRIORITIES

The Bible makes it clear that it is sin for money to become too important to us. We get into trouble when we value things improperly, getting our priorities wrong. Possessions, in any amount, come with certain dangers. Living wisely involves avoiding those dangers. Consider four dangers of money.

First, Proverbs 11:28 expresses *the danger of misplaced trust*. That verse says, "Whoever trusts in his riches will fall, but the righteous will flourish like a green leaf." Putting our trust in riches leads to a fall. It is misplaced trust. Where is your trust? Is your trust in God and his ability to take care of you? Or is your trust in your ability to make money? If we have any hope of living wisely, we have to be honest about what is in our hearts. Imagining that we trust God when we *don't* trust God is hardly the basis for a wise life. Some people *say* they trust God, but they don't obey God in the area of giving because they're *afraid* to give generously. The reason they're afraid is that money has become a source of security for them. They are trusting in money, not God. Do you feel more secure when you have more money in the bank, and less secure when you have less money in the bank? If so, then your sense of security is derived from money, not from

God. "Whoever trusts in his riches will fall, but the righteous will flourish."

A second danger of money is *the danger of prioritizing the temporary*. Possessions wear out; they are temporary. Therefore, it's foolish to prioritize money. According to a *Wall Street Journal* article by Robert Frank, a woman living in New York City posted an ad on Craigslist in the summer of 2007. She was advertising herself. She described herself as "spectacularly beautiful" and said she was looking for a husband who earned at least $500,000 per year. She had tried dating men who made around $250,000 per year, but that had not satisfied her. Her ad inspired all sorts of replies, one of which was posted by an investment banker. The banker pointed out that his money would grow over time, but her beauty would fade. Her offer wasn't good business, he said, since she was a "depreciating asset."[1] That must have hurt. But the man had a point. Physical things wear out; they're temporary. Of course, his point was an incomplete truth; his money may appreciate in the short term, but one day it's going to go away too.

Proverbs 23:4–5 says, "Do not toil to acquire wealth; be discerning enough to desist. When your eyes light on it, it is gone, for suddenly it sprouts wings, flying like an eagle toward heaven." Wealth is passing, temporary. It has wings. Whatever we own, in whatever amount, is going to spread wings and fly away one day. Why would any sane person prioritize something that is temporary when we could prioritize the eternal? Doesn't it make sense to invest our lives in something that's going to last? "Eat, drink, and be merry, for tomorrow we die" is one of the devil's oldest lies. First of all, merely eating and drinking doesn't lead to happiness; they don't satisfy because we are more than bodies. Second, tomorrow we don't die. We live forever somewhere, and we'll have to give an account for what we loved and trusted. In light of that, it's amazing that so many people live day after day and hardly ever think about eternal things.

B. H. Carroll was the founding president of Southwestern Baptist Theological Seminary. I read that, one time, he was traveling on a train, and a young man was sitting in the same compartment. Dr. Carroll asked the young man where he was going. The young man said that he was going to college. "What are you going to do then?" Dr. Carroll asked him. "After graduating from college, I'm going to law school." "What are you going to do then?" "After law school, I plan to get married." "What are you going to do then?" "I plan to have children and raise a family." "What are you going to do then?" The young man was a little annoyed at that point, and he said, "Well, I guess I'll grow old and die." "What are you going to do then?" And the young man said, "Well, I guess I haven't really thought much about that." The young man had made all his plans for time, but none for eternity. Think of the billions and billions of years we're going to spend in eternity, and compare that with the eighty or ninety years we may have here on earth—and then remember that we never know when we may die. Isn't it foolish to make our plans and expend our energies on this life instead of the life to come? Meditate on the wisdom of Proverbs 23:4–5, "Do not toil to acquire wealth. ... When your eyes light on it, it is gone." It has wings, and it's going to fly away.

A third danger of wealth is *the danger of pride*. Proverbs 30:8–9 is a prayer of the teacher of wisdom: "Give me neither poverty nor riches." So, the writer of Proverbs didn't want to be poor, but he didn't want to be rich either. Why didn't he want to be rich? This is his answer: "Give me neither poverty nor riches; feed me with the food that is needful for me, lest I be full and deny you and say, 'Who is the LORD?'"

It's a common trap. We're consumed with the desire to have more. We begin to have a love of money, which is evident from the amount of time we spend thinking about it and working for it. Then, when we begin to reach some financial goals, we swell with pride and think, "Look what I did." It's a great temptation for people who have some money to think too highly of themselves. That's why Paul wrote to Pastor Timothy, "As for the rich in this present age, charge them not to be haughty, nor to set their hopes on the uncertainty of riches, but on God, who richly provides us with everything to enjoy. They are to do good, to be rich in good works, to be generous and ready to share" (1 Tim 6:17–18). It's a danger of having money; we can so easily become proud.

A final danger is *the danger of looking to money for happiness.* What a tragedy to look for happiness from something that cannot give happiness. A desire to find happiness in money doesn't lead to happiness; it only leads to dissatisfaction. In Ecclesiastes 5:10, wise and wealthy Solomon wrote, "He who loves money will not be satisfied with money."

The book of Proverbs says that money has limited value. It's not nearly as valuable as righteousness, justice, or the fear of the Lord. Proverbs 15:16 says, "Better is a little with the fear of the LORD than great treasure and trouble with it." Many people think the opposite is true. They would say, "Having great treasure is a *lot* better than having a little; are you kidding?" But Proverbs 15:16 says that what's *really* valuable is the fear of the Lord, so the fear of the Lord plus a little equals more than great treasure, and sometimes great treasure just leads to trouble anyway. At a party, a man was admiring a lady's diamond pendant; it was an enormous diamond. He said, "That diamond must be a famous diamond, like the Hope Diamond." "No," she said, "It's the Klopman diamond. It's not famous, but like the Hope Diamond it comes with a curse." "Oh? What's the curse of the Klopman diamond?" The lady said, "Mr. Klopman." Money does not bring happiness. "Better is a little with the fear of the LORD than great treasure and trouble with it."

Let's close this chapter on money by thinking about Proverbs 11:4, which says, "Riches do not profit in the day of wrath, but righteousness delivers from death." Many people love money and accumulate money their entire lives, and they die without knowing Christ and finally learn that "riches do not profit in the day of wrath." On earth, sometimes money can be used to bribe a judge or "fix" a traffic ticket, but no amount of money will bribe heaven's Judge. So, on what basis will the Judge of the universe give us eternal life? "Riches do not profit in the day of wrath, but righteousness delivers from death." On the day when we stand before God in judgment, we won't need riches; we'll need righteousness. The Bible tells us the kind of righteousness we need. Isaiah 64:6 says, "All our righteous deeds are like a polluted garment." Our own righteousness amounts to dirty, useless rags. We need the righteousness of Christ that God gives to us when we put our faith in him. As Paul wrote in Philippians 3:9, "Not having a righteousness of my own that comes from the law, but that which comes through faith in Christ, the righteousness from God that depends on faith." When we place our faith in Christ, he gives us his righteousness, and on the merits of Christ's righteousness we have eternal life. We also have the presence of Christ in us, and he illuminates our minds to see the truth in his word. We begin to see everything, including wealth, with eyes that have been enlightened by divine wisdom. That's living well.

QUESTIONS FOR
REFLECTION

1. Think about your purchases over the last two months. Does any of your spending reflect vanity?

2. What's your coveting quotient? When you think about what you want, is it more money and stuff, or more of what matters most?

3. If someone looked at all your expenditures in the last year, would they conclude that you are generous?

CHAPTER 9

WORK:
"A VERY SACRED MATTER"

Robert Frost once said, "The world is full of will-ing people, some willing to work, the rest willing to let them."[1] Maybe you know someone who is willing to let others work. Frost's bit of wisdom reminds me of a story I once heard about a football team that was losing a game miserably. The other team had been scoring at will, and the first team had not even approached the goal line. They huddled up for a play near the end of the game and discovered that they had twelve players instead of eleven. They were already so embarrassed at the score that they didn't want to send somebody to the sideline and admit that they didn't have the correct number of players on the field. So, the quarter-back said, "Let's run a play next to the sideline, and one of us will just drop out and they'll never discover that we had too many players." So, they ran the play over to the sideline, but when they returned to the huddle only six men showed up.

Frost was right. The world is full of willing people, and a lot of them are willing to let others do the work. That's true in families, church, work, and school.

Nathan Hatch wrote an insightful article about our relationship to work that emphasizes its importance to us:

> Professional struggles touch the most sensitive nerves—regret in the wake of difficult decisions, disquiet at the lack of tangible accomplishment, stress from interpersonal conflict. ... Rarely are our souls sheltered from the storms that arise on the vocational horizon. ... Our sense of well-being often flows out of our professional standing or our career goal. Rightly or wrongly, our fondest hopes are wrapped up in professional identity. ...
>
> It is your law firm, your medical practice, your management-training group that consumes your waking hours and exacts your creative energies. Your profession tells you when to get up in the morning, what neighborhood to live in, what to wear to work, and where to "do lunch." Professional cultures define the meaning of success and acceptable standards of conduct. And, in all likelihood, you form close friendships with those who toil in the same professional vineyard.[2]

Hatch's words have to do with professional labor, but they apply to all kinds of labor. Working as a homemaker, a manual laborer, a student, a part-time worker, or a parent also touches sensitive nerves that go to the heart of our identity and well-being. Our work takes up so much of our time and energy, physical and emotional, that it should be clear that it's important to get it right, to do it wisely. Once again, the book of Proverbs, God's guide to living well, comes to our rescue.

YES, WORK IS POSITIVE
(THOUGH NOT VERY POPULAR)

Proverbs 6:9–11 says,

> How long will you lie there, O sluggard?
> When will you arise from your sleep?
> A little sleep, a little slumber,
> a little folding of the hands to rest,
> and poverty will come upon you like a robber,
> and want like an armed man.

Those verses are a few of the many in the book of Proverbs that describe the alternative to work—laziness—and laziness is soundly condemned in God's book of wisdom. Proverbs 6:9–11 also describes the consequences of laziness—poverty, need. That too is affirmed numerous times in Proverbs. Consider Proverbs 10:4–5:

> A slack hand causes poverty,
> but the hand of the diligent makes rich.
> He who gathers in summer is a prudent son,
> but he who sleeps in harvest is a son who brings shame.

Again, the consequence of laziness (or "a slack hand") is poverty. Two caveats should be added to verse 4. First, "rich" does not mean the same thing people in the modern West mean when they use that word. When we say "rich" we are referring to having millions of dollars in the bank. The ancient Near Eastern economy, on the other hand, was agrarian and pastoral, and to be rich was to have more livestock and land than one needed to survive. It meant having an abundant harvest. It meant living without the fear of imminent poverty.

Second, verse 4 illustrates the difference between a proverb and an absolute promise. Some lazy people are extraordinarily rich. Perhaps they inherited a fortune or won a lottery. Other people work hard and struggle financially. So, this and other proverbs concerning work and its consequent blessings are not absolute promises; they are statements that express general truths about life and provide guidance for living. In this case, the truth is that when we don't work, we suffer want, and when we work, we have enough. That's not only true, but it also helps us live well. It would hardly be wise to tell someone, "People have become insanely rich by winning the lottery. Therefore, the best way to live is to buy lottery tickets." That's foolish advice, since the odds of winning the lottery are smaller than the odds of getting hit by lightning. On the other hand, it is almost unalterably true that when we work hard we have enough. As someone once said, "The man who rolls up his sleeves is rarely in danger of losing his shirt." Proverbs tells us to roll up our sleeves.

Proverbs 10:4–5 warns of another consequence of laziness—shame. It's shameful to sleep in harvest. When the harvest is ripe and it's time to reap, it's shameful to sleep instead of work. The book of Proverbs provides all kinds of negative characteristics of lazy persons. One man was asked, "How long have you been working here?" He said, "Ever since the boss told me he'd fire me if I didn't get to work." Maybe you've heard of that sign in the road that says "Men Working Ahead ... We Hope."

The book of Proverbs provides numerous descriptions of lazy persons, and the descriptions are not at all flattering. For example, consider the following verses:

1. A lazy person may have irrational anxiety: "The sluggard says, 'There is a lion outside! I shall be killed in the streets!'" (22:13; see also 26:13).

2. A lazy person may choose to pursue what is empty instead of working: "Whoever works his land will have plenty of bread, but he who follows worthless pursuits lacks sense" (12:11).

3. A lazy person may resort to trying to gain wealth by get-rich-quick schemes, or by crime: "Wealth gained hastily will dwindle, but whoever gathers little by little will increase it" (13:11).

4. A lazy person damages projects and relationships more than he helps: "Whoever is slack in his work is a brother to him who destroys" (18:9).

5. A lazy person is wise in his own eyes: "The sluggard is wiser in his own eyes than seven men who can answer sensibly" (26:16).

6. A lazy person will be forced to borrow from others when he discovers too late that his negligence has left him without resources: "The sluggard does not plow in the autumn; he will seek at harvest and have nothing" (20:4).

7. A lazy person loves sleep, but he may not be able to sleep: "As a door turns on its hinges, so does a sluggard on his bed" (26:14). (A lazy person turns in bed like a door on its hinges, back and forth. A door never gets off its hinges; it just turns in the same place. The point is that a sluggard turns in bed but doesn't get out of bed.)

The book of Proverbs also says that a lazy person will be a nuisance to the one for whom he works. Proverbs 10:26 provides a vivid word picture: "Like vinegar to the teeth and smoke to the eyes, so is the sluggard to those who send him." Smoke is irritating to the eyes, and so is a lazy person to the one for whom he works. Vinegar is irritating to the teeth if you have enough of it in your mouth.

A few years after my wife and I were married, I went deer hunting with some friends, and one of the guys killed a deer. After he cleaned the deer, he gave me some of the meat. My wife is an outstanding cook, but at the time she had never cooked venison. She mentioned that fact to some ladies in our church, and she received multiple extemporaneous lessons in how to cook deer meat. She learned that everyone has their own recipe—all of them are different, and all of them have their own "secret." One lady told her that it's best to soak the meat in vinegar for a long time. However, she neglected to tell her to drain all the vinegar before cooking. So, my wife soaked the meat in vinegar and then cooked it in the vinegar. It tasted a lot like ... vinegar. Actually, it was like drinking straight vinegar. We made a valiant effort to eat it, but we were unsuccessful. Even using huge amounts of ketchup didn't help. The sour burn was just too strong. It made this verse come alive for us: "Like vinegar to the teeth and smoke to the eyes, so is the sluggard to those who send him." Yes, a lazy person who doesn't do what he's sent to do is truly irritating. To realize just how irritating a lazy person is, all I have to do is remember that vinegar-soaked venison—"like vinegar to the teeth."

A lot of people see work as a necessary evil—something they endure but will never enjoy. They think heaven will be an eternity of turning off the alarm clock and going back to sleep. When I was a child, I read that Abraham Lincoln worked hard in his growing-up years. As an adult, I read his words: "My father taught me to work, but not to love it. I never did like to work, and I don't deny it. I'd rather read, tell stories, crack jokes, talk, laugh—anything but work."

Work is not popular. Nevertheless, the biblical perspective of work is that work is positive, not negative. The Bible describes work as good and meaningful. It's true that one of the results of the original sin in the garden of Eden was that humanity now works the land and eats its fruit with toil and sweat, but work was present before the fall. Life in the garden of Eden was God's plan for a perfect life, and that life included work. Obviously, God thinks of work as positive. Yes, work is difficult sometimes, as a result of the fall, but it is still good and part of God's plan for us.

Suppose you won a lottery. First, everyone who knows you would be astonished, since they *know* you don't gamble, right? After you recovered from the shock, you would realize that you have instantly become a multimillionaire. You don't have to work anymore to put food on the table, or to pay for the kids' college. All your needs are met. Still, if you didn't work, you would be a sluggard, a lazy person. If you quit your job, you would have to find something productive to do through which you could work and make a contribution to God's world and the lives of others. In the garden of Eden, God met all the needs Adam and Eve had. Still, his plan for them included work.

Proverbs 14:23 says, "In all toil there is profit." During my growing-up years, I probably would not have believed that statement. My father was always a hard worker. As a young man he had also been a coach. He drilled the ethic of hustle and extra effort into his players. He also drilled it into his son. He made sure I always had work to do. I worked in the yard. He bought some land behind our yard, and we worked to clear that land and plant a garden. Then, we cleared more land and expanded the garden. He and I cleared the land and broke the ground by hand. In the years following, my father made sure I had regular chores in the garden. As a teenager, I had a man-ual-labor job and was involved in sports, but much of my free time was devoted to more work in the garden. I never enjoyed it. But I learned to work, and that lesson proved to be valu-able to me in the years that followed. When I was in college, I worked part-time jobs and still managed to make the dean's list. After marriage, I attended graduate school during the day and worked on the dock in New Orleans at night to support my wife and our first child. While serving as a full-time pas-tor of a church, I earned a PhD. That PhD. enabled me to fulfill my dream, and God's call, to teach Old Testament and Hebrew in graduate school. What would I be doing, where would I be, if I had not learned the value of hard work? I cite my own story not to boast about my accomplishments but to confess my foolishness. How foolish I was as a young person to think that my father was torturing me by making me work. Actually, he was giving me a great gift. He was teaching me the truth of Proverbs 14:23, "In all toil there is profit."

WORK IS PROVIDENTIAL

One of the reasons our work is profitable is that God works providentially in our labor. Many people find it difficult to see God at work in an exciting way at their jobs. Thomas Naylor wrote that "the average U.S. worker ... resents the authoritarian management style of his superiors. He has no motivation to work hard at his job. He is ... suffering from alienation—from his work, his co-workers, his family."[3] "Resents," "no motivation," and "suffering from alienation"—what a negative picture of "the average U.S. worker." Evidently, a lot of people are not excited about their work.

It's easy to get into a routine in which we are awakened by the alarm clock, push the snooze button to get that all-important extra ten minutes of sleep, then stagger to the kitchen, gulp down same caffeine and choke down some toast, run out the door, fight the traffic, arrive at work to go through the routine, then go home, putter around the house, put the mind in neutral and watch TV, and go to bed. For many people, it's the same rut all week long, every week, like a treadmill—nothing exciting, nothing different, certainly nothing meaningful. It seems so monotonous and meaningless.

Think about this: your work is meaningful and providential because *God put you where you work*. Okay, I know. Some of you are thinking, "Well, Allan, maybe God called you to your work—you're a writer, a seminary professor, and a preacher"—but I don't believe God had much to do with my job. I'm working there because it was the best job I could get at the time, and I continue to work there so that my family can eat." A lot of people would like to be in a job where they believe that God called them, but they just don't see that it has ever happened.

This may surprise you, but God may have placed you where you are, and you may not be aware of it. Proverbs 16:9 says, "The heart of man plans his way, but the LORD establishes his steps." God is involved in the circumstances of our lives, sometimes even overruling our own plans. Proverbs 20:24 says, "A man's steps are from the LORD." That's the reason I used the word "providential"—God exercises his sovereignty by working in our lives in ways that are above and beyond what we may realize, and for reasons we don't know at the time.

Consider the Bible's description of Joseph. Joseph was sold into slavery against his will by his brothers. In Egypt, he experienced hardship, slavery, and imprisonment. What was his job? He was a slave in the house of Potiphar. Potiphar was important; Joseph was not. Then, Joseph was wrongly accused of a crime and sent to prison. No earthly status could be lower, except for death. Still, even in prison, Joseph prospered. Genesis 39:21–23 says,

> The LORD was with Joseph and showed him steadfast love and gave him favor in the sight of the keeper of the prison. And the keeper of the prison put Joseph in charge of all the prisoners who were in the prison. Whatever was done there, he was the one who did it. The keeper of the prison paid no attention to anything that was in Joseph's charge, because the LORD was with him. And whatever he did, the LORD made it succeed.

Why did Joseph prosper? "Because the LORD was with him," and "The LORD made [him] succeed." God was with him and was blessing him, even in prison.

When Joseph's brothers sold him into slavery, or when he was sent to prison, I seriously doubt he would have said, "This is God's will for my life. God has called me to be a slave and prisoner in Egypt." But later, looking back on God's providential work in his life, he was able to see that God had his hand in it all along. Genesis 45:8 says that Joseph said to his brothers, "It was not you who sent me here, but God."

Consider also the Jews in the time of Jeremiah. They watched Jerusalem be destroyed and their beloved temple burned to the ground. After that, they were exiled to Babylon against their will. Here's what the Lord said to them in Babylon through his prophet Jeremiah:

> Thus says the Lord of hosts ... to all the exiles whom I *have sent* into exile from Jerusalem to Babylon: ... "Seek the welfare of the city where I have sent you into exile, and pray to the Lord on its behalf." (Jer 29:4, 7)

Babylon was not where they wanted to be. It would not even have made the top-ten list. Psalm 137 says that in Babylon they cried out, "How shall we sing the Lord's song in a foreign land?" (v. 4). They wanted to go back to Jerusalem. But God said, "I've put you there, even though it's not where you want to be. Seek the welfare of that place, and pray for the people there."

Maybe God is saying that to someone reading this chapter. Maybe you're facing difficult circumstances in your labor, like Joseph. Maybe you're not where you want to be, like the Jews in Babylon. Don't be so quick to say, "I'm not called to this job." Remember Proverbs 16:9—"The heart of man plans his way, but the Lord establishes his steps." Proverbs 20:24 says, "A man's steps are from the Lord." God has providentially allowed you to be where you are. Maybe God is calling you to go somewhere else, and if he is, by all means go, but in the meantime God may have you where you are for reasons you cannot see. Approach work as providential because God put you where you work.

Also, our work is providential because *God provides work.* Remember that Proverbs 14:23 says, "In all toil there is profit." Also, remember that work was part of God's perfect environment before sin entered the world. Genesis 2:15 says, "The LORD God took the man and put him in the garden of Eden to work it and keep it." Couldn't God have cared for that garden without Adam's help? Of course! He created the garden from nothing, so he certainly could have cut the grass and pruned the fruit trees. But God chose to give to humanity the task of caring for his world. He chose to invite us to be his partners in managing his creation. That's what work is—it's working with God to care for his world. We're partners and employees in "Care for the World, Inc." The owner and CEO of the company is God.

A teenager who was working at a fast-food restaurant once told me that he couldn't wait to quit his job. I asked him, "Why?" He said, "I want to do something that's at least a little important, and let's face it, flipping burgers is not an important job." I told him that I disagreed, and he asked me why. I said, "Don't people have to eat?" He said, "Yes." I asked him, "Do you think *God* wants people to have food to eat?" He said, "Yes." I said, "Well, since it's the will of God for people to eat, you're doing the will of God to get food to the people God created and loves. Farmers grew and harvested the food, so they were God's instruments to provide food for people. Truck drivers transported the food. God used them to get the food to the restaurants. Somebody has to cook the food and sell it to the people, and that's you. You're working with God to care for his creation, and that's noble work." Thinking about flipping burgers as noble work may be countercultural, but it is absolutely biblical, and it's part of living well.

For hundreds of years the church saw the work of priests and monks as more sacred than so-called secular work. However, during the Reformation, the Reformers strongly rejected that distinction. Martin Luther expressed it this way:

> It looks like a great thing when a monk renounces everything and goes into a cloister, carries on a life of asceticism, fasts, watches, prays, etc. ... On the other hand, it looks like a small thing when a maid cooks and cleans and does other housework. But because God's command is there, even such a small work must be praised as a service of God far surpassing the holiness and asceticism of all monks and nuns. ... Your work is a very sacred matter. God delights in it, and through it He wants to bestow His blessing on you. This praise of work should be inscribed on all tools, on the forehead and the face that sweat from toiling.[4]

"Your work is a very sacred matter. God delights in it." We should never think that work is punishment for sin. The home in which Jesus grew up was the home of a man who worked with his hands. Jesus surely helped his father to do the work of a carpenter. Whether Jesus was mending plows or mending souls, he was doing the work of God. Why? Because God created and cares about people, and people have to have houses to live in, furniture to sit on, food to eat, and clothes to wear. When we work to provide for people, we're participating in God's plan to provide for his creation as much as Adam was doing so when he tilled the garden.

Three men were laying bricks for a building. Someone asked them what they were doing. One of them said, "I'm working for x number of dollars an hour." The second man said, "I'm laying bricks." The third man said, "I'm building a great cathedral for people to come and worship God." All honorable and honest work can be seen as participating with God in caring for his world and making it a better place. Our work is providential because God put us where we work, and God provided our work.

WORK IS A PLATFORM

Let's return to Nathan Hatch's article on working as a Christian in a profession. He wrote:

> Professional life rewards good work. Unfortunately, this reinforces a sense that success is the measure of all. The professions are a meritocracy: an accurate diagnosis leads to a successful cure; a sound legal argument wins a case; a correct design makes a bridge withstand traffic. The professions reward competence and penalize incompetence. Who can argue with that? But success easily becomes the measuring stick for evaluating people. Life becomes a balance sheet of merit and reward. We applaud success in ourselves; and we rank other people accordingly. The professions reinforce our love of being winners. All too soon, professionals get to the top of the heap, congratulate themselves, and look down on others.[5]

In other words, the inevitable meritocracy of labor in a free enterprise system is both good and bad. It "rewards good work." That's good. It also creates a mindset, a culture that measures people by their professional or financial success. That's bad. God's book of wisdom says that there are other, more important, ways of measuring people. Of greatest importance—do they fear God? Second, are they simple, wise, or foolish?

For God's people, work is a platform because we have the opportunity to interact with other people and influence them to fear God and develop wisdom. Many of God's people love and want to serve God, but they have the idea that the only time they can serve God is when they are away from their secular jobs. The result is that they give God some spare time at church, but their "nonsacred" career gets the most and best hours. They are compartmentalizing their lives so that one compartment is God's part—Sunday, church work, tithing—and the other compartment is the secular part and is not ministry. But dividing life into two parts—sacred and secular—is not the goal of the wise person.

God's way of living well includes realizing that even "secular" labor is, as Martin Luther put it, "a very sacred matter." For the people of God, life is not divided into two or three parts. All of life is under the lordship of the one true God and is therefore sacred. The second chapter of Ephesians affirms that we are reconciled to God by his grace, not by our good works. We cannot do enough good things to earn a relationship with God and eternal life in heaven. We can only turn from sin, put our faith in Jesus, and be given the gifts of reconciliation to God and eternal life. Then, Ephesians 2:10 describes the result of being made new in Christ. It says, "We are his workmanship, created in Christ Jesus for good works." Once we are recreated in Christ, we are God's workmanship, his works of art. The result is that we do good works. So, we don't do good works in order to be reconciled to God; we do good works because he has saved us and transformed us. Our good works are the consequences of being God's workmanship. And there is no realm of life in which we cease to be his workmanship. We are "created in Christ Jesus for good works," whether we're at home, at work, or at church. So, on our jobs, we're serving God, as *his* workmanship.

Think about the place where you work or go to school as you read what Jesus said in Matthew 5:14–16:

> You are the light of the world. A city set on a hill cannot be hidden. Nor do people light a lamp and put it under a basket, but on a stand, and it gives light to all in the house. In the same way,

let your light shine before others, so that they
may see your good works and give glory to your
Father who is in heaven.

Jesus said that his followers are to shine the light of their
good works. It's what we do, wherever we are. We do good
works, other people see our good works, and they give glory
to the God who saved us and made us new. All God's people are
serving God full-time somewhere. The Bible does not teach
that we serve God in worship but do something else during
the week. He is Lord over all of life. We belong to him all the
time. Everything we do, including work, is for him.

So, our work is a platform for ministry because of our relationship with God. It's also a platform for ministry because
of our relationships with our coworkers. Some people think,
"I would have no problem seeing my work as a platform for
ministry if I worked at a church where everybody is always
smiling, praying, and praising God, and nobody does or says
anything wrong. But if I'm not going to work in a church, at
least I could work in a Christian company, or surrounded by
Christians. The people with whom I work tell dirty stories and
take the Lord's name in vain and gossip. They're materialistic
and self-centered. If I could only get out of this place, I could
serve God!" To the contrary, God may have put you in that specific place with those specific people because that's where a
Christian witness is needed more than anywhere else.

Consider the example of Daniel. Daniel was a Jew who
was exiled to Babylon. He was placed in a job against his will
in a pagan nation. He was surrounded by people who didn't
know God. In fact, they were idolaters. He had to work for the
very government that was the bitter enemy of God's people.
But Daniel didn't believe, "When in Babylon, do as the Baby-
lonians." They tried to force him into their lifestyle, and they
forbade him to pray, but Daniel stayed faithful to God. So they
threw him to the lions. You may have suffered persecution

on the job, but I'll bet you've never been thrown into a lions' den. But what did Daniel do? He just pulled up a lion for a pillow, pulled out his Old Testament, and began to "read between the lions"! The next morning the king came to check on Daniel and called out to him, "Daniel, servant of the living God, has your God, *whom you serve continually*, been able to deliver you from the lions?" (Dan 6:20). God *had* delivered him, but did you notice what the king said about Daniel? The king said Daniel had been serving God continually. Daniel had a secular job among idolatrous people, but even his enemies who didn't know God had to admit that his secular job was really sacred, because he was serving God.

What was the result of Daniel's service? The king said about God, whom Daniel had been serving, "He is the living God, enduring forever; his kingdom shall never be destroyed" (Dan 6:26). Those words were spoken by a king who had never known God. How would he ever have known the power of God had it not been for Daniel, who had a secular job in circumstances that were anything but ideal but who used it as an opportunity to serve God? It's easy for us to want to get out of Babylon, but God needs Daniels in Babylon to show his power and glory.

Paul wrote in Philippians 2:15 that Christians are to live as "children of God without blemish in the midst of a crooked and twisted generation, among whom you shine as lights in the world." Daniel did that, and so should we. Jesus said in John 20:21, "As the Father has sent me, even so I am sending you." The Father sent Jesus from the glories of heaven to the suffering of earth for the salvation of lost people. Jesus sends his followers on that same mission—from the safety of the church to a crooked and twisted world to seek and to save those who are lost. His people are more than laborers, salesmen, teachers, lawyers, homemakers, doctors, executives, retirees, and students. We are ambassadors for Christ to people who are lost in sin. We are people to whom God has given his radical wisdom, and we're to call others around us to fear him and learn his wisdom. That's a very sacred matter.

QUESTIONS FOR REFLECTION

1. Would the way you work change if you viewed your work more positively? How so?
2. Why do you think God, in his providence, has you doing the work you currently do?
3. Name at least three ways you can serve God in your present job.
4. Specifically, what can you do where you work that will cause you to stand out as a light for Christ?

CHAPTER 10

SEDUCTION OF A SIMPLETON

Y EARS AGO, I PREPARED A BIBLE STUDY ON THE SUBJECT OF sexual sin for a weeknight prayer meeting. I decided to teach on that subject because the book of Proverbs addresses it, and I was teaching from Proverbs. As the evening to present the study approached, I felt foolish. I was about to talk about sexual sin to a group of people who were gathering during the week for a prayer meeting. Of all the people in the world, that group was the least likely to need a message about sexual sin. Nevertheless, I had prepared the study, and I presented it. After the meeting was over, a man came up to me and said, "I'm really glad you taught on that subject tonight; it's really needed." A few minutes later another man said to me, "Thanks for talking about that tonight; you don't know how much it's needed."

Have you ever had the feeling that someone was telling you something important but you had no idea what it was? I thought that topic was irrelevant to that group of people, but those two men were telling me otherwise. What they knew, and I was later to learn, was that one of the men in the group that night was involved in an extramarital affair.

It saddens me deeply to write that at this point in my life I have seen and heard far too much to think that a message on sexual sin is not needed in the church, in any meeting. Teaching on that topic is needed first of all because God has said something about it in his Word, and we ought to listen to what he says. Second, the devil constantly bombards us with his lies about sex. Television shows portray over a thousand acts of sexual contact per year, and the overwhelming majority of that contact is outside marriage. The people around us regularly contradict what God says in his word by what they say and what they do. Many Americans do not believe premarital sex is a sin. Not surprisingly, then, many of them are having premarital and extramarital sex. It is not an exaggeration to say that we live in a culture that is obsessed with sex. The saddest fact is the extent to which the church of Jesus Christ is being influenced by the culture. Randy Alcorn has summarized the situation well: "Nothing so hamstrings the believer's spiritual potency as sexual compromise—and never has the church in America been so compromised as now."[1]

The moral degeneration in our culture has had devastating effects on personal morality and family stability. Even Christians are being deceived into thinking, "Well, maybe I *can* commit sexual sin without any negative consequences," or "Maybe it's really not that bad to do what God's word says not to do." A young man and young woman came to my office to talk. Both of them said that they were Christians, though when the young lady found out what a Christian is she realized she wasn't a Christian, and she prayed to receive Christ. This young man and woman were living together outside of marriage. I told them that they should not be doing that. They said, "Well, our parents always told us that this is wrong, but they never told us why. Their generation didn't do this, but a lot of people are doing it now. Does the Bible really say that living together is wrong? What *does* the Bible say about living together?" I turned to 1 Thessalonians 4:3–5, and read to them,

> This is the will of God, your sanctification: that
> you abstain from sexual immorality; that each
> one of you know how to control his own body
> in holiness and honor, not in the passion of lust
> like the Gentiles who do not know God.

God's will is our sanctification, and with it, our abstinence from sexual immorality. I also shared with that couple a few of the things in this chapter. Let's consider God's wisdom concerning sex under four headings. I think this wisdom from Proverbs will answer the questions posed by that couple in my office, plus a few other questions. I know it will help us to live well.

RESERVE AFFECTION FOR YOUR SPOUSE

Christians who say that sex outside of marriage is wrong are sometimes considered prudes, and God is portrayed as anti-sex. Actually, God invented sex. He is the one who first thought of it, and he gave it to the first man and woman, whom he also created.

A fundamental question here does not have to do specifically with sex. It has to do with authority. Who has the right, the authority, to establish the standards concerning sexuality (or absence of standards)? For those who consider the Old Testament the word of God, the God who created us possesses that right, especially since he has much to say about the subject in his word. Therefore, faithful Jews and Christians are not willing to normalize what God has proscribed. The one who created us has the right to establish the standards. Only knowing and following his pattern will lead to health and happiness.

Proverbs 18:22 reflects God's pattern: "He who finds a wife finds a good thing and obtains favor from the LORD."

Notice that "wife" and "good" are in synonymous parallelism. A *wife* is equated to *good*. That's reminiscent of the creation. When God made the first man, without a wife, he announced, "It is not good that the man should be alone; I will make a helper fit for him" (Gen 2:18). When man was alone, it was "not good." When a man finds a wife, it's "good." It's good to have a wife (or husband). That doesn't minimize the legitimacy of singleness, which the Bible affirms (1 Cor 7:7–9). Nevertheless, it underscores that marriage is a God-ordained benefit.

Proverbs 18:22 further emphasizes the blessing of marriage by stating that when a man finds a wife he "obtains favor from the LORD." In other words, marriage pleases God. Also, the wife herself is God's gift, the expression of his favor. The book of Proverbs acknowledges that all wives are not blessings (12:4; 21:9; 27:15). Still, following God's pattern of marriage is good and pleasing to him.

The definition of "family" is undergoing a metamorphosis in contemporary Western culture. However, God's blueprint for the family, revealed in Scripture, does not change. His plan is for one man to marry one woman for life. The Bible contains stories about men who had more than one wife, but the Bible contains no statement that God condoned it. He revealed his plan when he said that a man should "hold fast to his wife" (not "wives"; Gen 2:24). One man is to cleave to his one wife. God even commanded his people not to *want* another woman (Exod 20:17). Furthermore, once a man and woman marry, God says that the marriage is permanent (Matt 19:4–9). God's people are to follow and honor God's way, since the Bible says, "Let marriage be held in honor among all" (Heb 13:4).

So, we honor the institution of marriage and our spouses. Proverbs 5:15–19 gives some practical guidance in how to do that, using vivid metaphorical language. It says,

> Drink water from your own cistern,
> flowing water from your own well.

Should your springs be scattered abroad,
streams of water in the streets?
Let them be for yourself alone,
and not for strangers with you.
Let your fountain be blessed,
and rejoice in the wife of your youth,
a lovely deer, a graceful doe.
Let her breasts fill you at all times with delight;
be intoxicated always in her love.

Those verses compare sex to water. Water is pleasurable, sat-
isfying, healthy, and necessary for life. All those things are
also true of sex. But anyone in his right mind will be careful
about the source of his water. Water is great, but water in a
mud puddle is *not* great, and it could hurt you. When we travel
internationally to some countries, people warn us, "Don't
drink the water." They're saying that to protect us. God says in
Proverbs, "Drink water from your own cistern, flowing water
from your own well." If you drink anything else, it's dangerous; it's not good for you. Just to make sure we don't miss the
point of the analogy, God makes it explicit: "Rejoice in the
wife of your youth. ... Be intoxicated always in *her* love." Looking for love anywhere else would be as dumb as going out in
the street and drinking water from a puddle. Drink "flowing
water from your own well."

God created sex for the marriage relationship. Outside
the marriage relationship it's dirty and contaminated. As a
young man I pastored a rural church, so we lived in a farm-
ing area. The soil of those fields was beautiful. We saw our
neighbors plow the dirt and plant, and then we watched the
plants grow and bear fruit. Dirt is a wonderful thing, in its
place. But if our farmer neighbors had thrown some of their
dirt in our house, we would have thought it was just ... dirty.
It would be ugly, out of place, and we would not regard our
house as clean until we removed it. In the same way, sex is

beautiful in its proper place, but outside of marriage it's dirty and wrong.

It comes as a surprise to some people that the Bible, in Proverbs 5 and elsewhere, encourages marital sex. In fact, 1 Corinthians 7:1-5 commands couples not to refuse one another this act of love. It says, "Do not deprive one another" (v. 5). I've read that passage to couples in premarital counseling, sometimes just for my own amusement. The young lady usually turns red with embarrassment, and the young man is like Gomer Pyle on the old *Andy Griffith Show*: "Shazam! I didn't know that was in the Bible!" It *is* in the Bible.

As William Frey has written,

> When we say no to promiscuity or other substitutes for marriage, we do so in defense of good sex. It is not from prudery that the Bible advocates lifelong, faithful, heterosexual marriage, but out of a conviction that the freedom and loving abandon that are necessary for sexual ecstasy come only from a committed marital relationship. ... Only the real thing really works.[2]

God is not trying to keep sex *from* us; he's trying to keep it *for* us. Sex is right and good only in the place God intended it—the marriage relationship. God knows all the pain people experience when they go outside the sexual boundaries he has established. He wants to help us avoid that pain so we can live well. Therefore, in his word he encourages us to pour out our affection on our own spouse.

DEVELOP AWARENESS OF THE WAYS OF THE SEXUALLY PROMISCUOUS

People who are promiscuous—willing to have sex with multiple people—used to be called "loose." The book of Proverbs warns of the ways of a loose woman. Of course, there are plenty of loose men too, but Proverbs was addressed primarily to young men preparing for leadership in adult life, so the warnings have to do with the dangers of having a relationship with a loose woman. If you want to make your marriage affair-proof, or if you want to avoid falling for any kind of sexual temptation, become a student of the book of Proverbs. It will make you wise, and wise people stay away from illicit sex. God inspired the writer of Proverbs 7 to describe what sexual temptation looks like, so we won't be surprised by it. Consider this detailed description of a typical incident of sexual temptation, as described by the wisdom teacher.

> My son, keep my words
> and treasure up my commandments with you;
> keep my commandments and live;
> keep my teaching as the apple of your eye;
> bind them on your fingers;
> write them on the tablet of your heart.
> Say to wisdom, "You are my sister,"
> and call insight your intimate friend,
> to keep you from the forbidden woman,
> from the adulteress with her smooth words.
> For at the window of my house
> I have looked out through my lattice,
> and I have seen among the simple,
> I have perceived among the youths,
> a young man lacking sense,
> passing along the street near her corner,
> taking the road to her house
> in the twilight, in the evening,
> at the time of night and darkness.
> And behold, the woman meets him,
> dressed as a prostitute, wily of heart.
> She is loud and wayward;
> her feet do not stay at home;
> now in the street, now in the market,

and at every corner she lies in wait.
She seizes him and kisses him,
and with bold face she says to him,
"I had to offer sacrifices,
and today I have paid my vows;
so now I have come out to meet you,
to seek you eagerly, and I have found you.
I have spread my couch with coverings,
colored linens from Egyptian linen;
I have perfumed my bed with myrrh,
aloes, and cinnamon.
Come, let us take our fill of love till morning;
let us delight ourselves with love.
For my husband is not at home;
he has gone on a long journey;
he took a bag of money with him;
at full moon he will come home."
With much seductive speech she persuades him;
with her smooth talk she compels him.
All at once he follows her,
as an ox goes to the slaughter,
or as a stag is caught fast
till an arrow pierces its liver;
as a bird rushes into a snare;
he does not know that it will cost him his life.
And now, O sons, listen to me,
and be attentive to the words of my mouth.
Let not your heart turn aside to her ways;
do not stray into her paths,
for many a victim has she laid low,
and all her slain are a mighty throng.
Her house is the way to Sheol,
going down to the chambers of death. (Prov 7:1–27)

The first way of tempting someone into sexual sin is *isolation*. The temptress of Proverbs 7 meets the young man "lacking sense" at night, when no one is around, and in the darkness, where no one can see (vv. 7–9). As if to emphasize the privacy of the setting, the writer of Proverbs 7 says essentially the same thing four times: "In the twilight, in the evening, at the time of night and darkness" (v. 9). The tempting woman further emphasizes secrecy when she tells the young simpleton, "My husband is not at home; he has gone on a long journey" (v. 19).

This is the way of those who attempt to entice someone into sexual sin. They don't stand up in a crowd and shout, "Billy, I would like to commit adultery with you! Let's go to my place and have illicit sex!" That's not what the wisdom teacher saw from the window of his house, and that's not the way it happens.

Instead, those who tempt with sexual sin specialize in isolation. They approach when no one else is around, when no one else can see. Why? Isolation creates the illusion of anonymity, secrecy. But it is an illusion. Secrecy is a major reason why so many people are drawn to using Internet pornography, but Internet activity also is not as secret as people think. In the case of the encounter described in Proverbs 7, the wisdom teacher saw what was happening, even though it was ostensibly in private. And whether another person sees or not, God *always* sees. Hebrews 4:13 says, "No creature is hidden from his sight, but all are naked and exposed to the eyes of him to whom we must give account." God not only sees, he also holds us accountable for what he sees. That alone should prevent us from engaging in sexual sin, even in isolation. Consider the following story from the life of Chuck Swindoll:

> I was in Canada. ... I had been away from home
> for eight days, and there were two more to go—

a weekend. I was lonely and having a pity party for myself at supper—alone. I bought a newspaper, thumbed through the sports section, and found nothing but hockey—the favorite of Canadians but not mine. I heaved a sigh and walked toward the elevator. En route, I heard a couple of young women talking and laughing. ... I smiled as I passed by and a few steps later punched the "up" elevator button. I got on. So did the two ladies. I punched "6." They didn't reach for the row of buttons, so I asked, "What floor?" One looked at me rather sensually and said, "How about six? Do you have any plans?" We were all alone on an elevator. In Canada. I was flattered to be honest. ... These women were available, and I was lonely. On that trip from the lobby to the sixth floor, I had an extremely significant decision to make. ... Do you know what immediately flashed into my mind? My wife and four children? No, not at first. My position and reputation? No, not then. The possibility of being seen or set up? No. God gave me an instant visual replay of Galatians 6:7: "Do not be deceived, God is not mocked; for whatever a man sows, this he will also reap." ... As I looked back at the two, I replied, "I've got a full evening planned already; I'm really not interested."³

A second way sensual people tempt is with *beauty*. Proverbs 6:25 says this about a sensually-minded woman: "Do not desire her beauty in your heart." Proverbs 7 describes the ways the adulteress adorned herself in order to entice— "dressed as a prostitute" (v. 10). Physical appearance is used all the time to attract people to sexual sin. It's no sin to look nice, it's no sin to be pretty or handsome, and there's nothing particularly spiritual about looking unkempt. On the other hand, one's looks should not be used in the wrong way. Beauty should never be the means of enticing to lust, which is sin. Proverbs 31:30 says, "Charm is deceitful, and beauty is vain, but a woman who fears the LORD is to be praised."

Men and ladies are attracted sexually by what they see. Therefore, it is imperative that godly women and men dress modestly. Wise people realize that their appearance is providing visual stimuli to those who see them, so they dress modestly lest they encourage lustful thoughts. Sometimes it takes extra effort to find something modest to wear, but it's worth the effort so we do not look as sensuous as our corrupt culture and tempt people to lust. Some people may resist such efforts, thinking, "I'm not responsible for what goes on in the minds of other people!" No, we are not. Still, we *are* responsible for what we put on our bodies. When we shop, it will help us to listen to the counsel of parents, other family members, and friends. Smart shoppers do that anyway. My wife and daughter help me pick out clothes all the time. "I think I'll get that tie." "No." "But I thought it would look good with ..." "No." I would be pretty dumb to ignore good advice.

If you don't have a wise person who is close enough to you to give you godly advice, then consider taking mine: Men, when we dress and prepare for the day, let's think about how we are going to help other people during that day, not how we are going to attract attention to ourselves or to our physical features. When we do that, we won't mind covering muscles instead of displaying them. Ladies, make sure your clothes are long enough at the bottom and high enough on top. And people of both genders should check their vanity at their closet door.

At the risk of wandering too far afield, I want to add three important postscripts to the discussion about dress and beauty. First, it is certainly possible to dress stylishly while dressing modestly. Some people do this by finding a role model—someone who always looks "put together" but never dresses immodestly. Second, references to covering our bodies are not meant to suggest that we are ashamed of the way God has created us; to the contrary, all of us should cultivate gratitude for the way God created our bodies and make an effort to take care of them to his glory. Part of marriage is accepting and loving one another's bodies the way they are. Third, remember that what we use to *catch* someone is what we'll have to use to *keep* that someone. If he or she is with you just because of your looks, what are you going to do when your skin begins to wrinkle, your hair turns gray, and the beauty of youth begins to fade? Pardon the pun, but your marriage will not be a pretty sight. If someone *is* dating you because of your looks, he or she doesn't deserve to be with you, so dump him or her, find somebody who wants to please God, and avoid a lifetime of heartache.

A third way sensuous people seduce is the use of *flattery*. As the wisdom teacher of Proverbs 7 watched from his window, he saw that "with much seductive speech she persuades him; with her smooth talk she compels him" (v. 21). Proverbs 5:3-4 says, "The lips of a forbidden woman drip honey, and her speech is smoother than oil, but in the end she is bitter as wormwood, sharp as a two-edged sword." Proverbs 6:24 also refers to "the smooth tongue of the adulteress." How big a fool some people become over people who flatter them. "You're so big and strong." "You're so beautiful." "You're so handsome." "You're so sexy." In the chapter having to do with our use of words, we saw that flattery is like perfume. It's all right to sniff it, but you're not supposed to swallow it. When swallowed, flattery can draw people into sexual sin. Believing flattery makes big fools of little people. We all like to be liked, and we love to be loved. So, flattery is like a powerful emotional drug. We long for the approval of others—

to be thought of as attractive, intelligent, important. Flattery seems to give us that, but it's phony. Sensual flatterers are lying; they're only using words to manipulate our emotions so we'll do what they want. It's actually cruel.

Furthermore, when someone tells us how wonderful we are, we are inclined to feel an emotional attraction to that person. It's obvious that the flatterer is really intelligent, since he or she sees how great we are! He or she also has a lot in common with us since we see things the same way! Thus, we are drawn into a relationship with the flatterer. Once we experience that powerful draw and emotional attachment, if the flatterer is also sexually promiscuous, we're sitting ducks for sexual temptation and sin.

Proverbs also mentions a fourth way of enticing to sexual sin—*a flirtatious face*. The watching wisdom teacher saw the seductive woman approach the young man "with bold face" (7:13). The NASB and the NIV use the word "brazen." The Hebrew phrase could be rendered literally, "she made her face strong." That explains the old Young's Literal Translation (YLT), "She hath hardened her face." But a "hard" face is hardly what the temptress used to entice the young sucker on the street corner. The woman "made her face strong" by preparing it and using it to provide the strongest possible temptation. That would inevitably include a seductive smile, a lingering stare, and flirtatious eyes. The latter is referred to explicitly in the second part of Proverbs 6:25. That verse also refers to a sensuous woman, and it says, "Do not let her capture you with her eyelashes." Today, people talk about a "come hither look," or "bedroom eyes."

We should all watch out for a face that intentionally tempts or entices. It dates back at least to the time of Solomon, and those batting eyelashes have been catching simpletons ever since. Guys interested in sexual sin also use their faces. He gives her that forlorn, puppy-dog look and says, "If you love me, let me." That's not love; it's lust. People don't have to have a physical relationship to prove love. Love involves mutual trust, respect, and appreciation for the other person's character. When somebody has real love, the last thing he or she wants to do is to ruin the purity of the beloved. Before the ultimate physical step is taken, the ultimate commitment ought to be made—that's marriage.

KNOW THE ARENA OF SEXUAL TEMPTATION

I once heard a pastor tell of an experience he had while traveling to preach in a church for the first time. He was running late, and to make matters worse, he got lost. Since he was so late, he knew that the service would begin before he arrived. He also knew that the sermon was not the first item on the order of worship, so his plan was to park quickly, run into the church, and walk straight to the podium so he would be in place before he was scheduled to preach. He did that and was delighted that he arrived before the time for the sermon. After a few minutes, someone on the church staff approached him and whispered something to him. He and the staff member quickly exited the podium and the worship center. Unfortunately, he had been sitting on the podium of the wrong church!

It does little good to march into battle only to arrive at the wrong battlefield. If we are serious about fighting the battle against sexual temptation, we have to locate the right battlefield. Where is that battle fought? Proverbs 4:23 says, "Keep your heart with all vigilance, for from it flow the springs of life." The first verses of Proverbs 7, cited above, state that the wisdom teacher exhorted the readers to keep his teaching on the tablet of our hearts, "to keep you from the forbidden woman, from the adulteress with her smooth words."

Today, when we refer to our hearts, we're referring to our emotions. "I heart my dog" means "I feel affection for my dog." For the Hebrews, the heart didn't only represent emotions;

it also represented thinking and deciding. A familiar phrase in the Hebrew Bible is "to set your heart" on something, and that meant to think about something, or to consider it carefully. The arena of sexual temptation is the thought life—our thinking. That's where Satan is launching his attack today, and the writer of Proverbs urges us to keep our hearts, since that's where the direction of our lives will be determined. "Keep your heart with all vigilance."

Filling our minds with God's wisdom for living well equips us to fight and win the warfare that is being waged in the arena of our minds. Psalm 119 says, "How can a young man keep his way pure? By guarding it according to your word. ... I have stored up your word in my heart, that I might not sin against you" (vv. 9, 11). We will remain pure if we win the war that is being waged in our minds, and we'll win that war if we're constantly filling our minds with God's wisdom.

When someone we know becomes involved in sexual sin, people often think, "Everything was going so well. He was in church every Sunday. Then *all of a sudden* this happened." Usually, it *doesn't* happen all of a sudden. Most of the time, the battle had been lost long before in the arena of the mind. The action was preceded by a thought—sometimes many thoughts over a long period of time until finally the opportunity arose to act.

This world and the god of this world are waging a war in the minds of people. On the other hand, God wants us to present our minds to him. When God molds someone to be like Jesus, he changes the way that person thinks. Romans 12:2 says, "Be transformed by the renewal of your mind." How are we transformed? We are changed when our minds are renewed. Our minds are renewed when we think according to what God says in his word, and we no longer think according to the ways of a sinful world. How do we think according to God's word? We program God's word into the computer of our minds by reading it daily, meditating on it, and memorizing it. There really are no shortcuts. Someone reading this may need a renewed mind. Go to God's wisdom in his word. Learn it, so you can say with the psalmist, "I have stored up your word in my heart, that I might not sin against you."

When we have renewed minds, we have built-in warning systems to protect us from temptation. We'll put temptation away as we think God's thoughts. We'll be able to say with Job, "I have made a covenant with my eyes" (Job 31:1), so sensual sights won't entice us. Our Christlike thinking will govern what we see. Lewd conversation and dirty jokes won't interest us. We'll have the wisdom to avoid going to places where we would be tempted. The battle will be won, or lost, in the arena of sexual temptation—our thinking. "Keep your heart with all vigilance."

REPEAT YOUR AFFIRMATION OF THE HARM OF SEXUAL SIN

Consider the words of Proverbs 6:32–33: "He who commits adultery lacks sense; he who does it destroys himself. He will get wounds and dishonor, and his disgrace will not be wiped away." Also, think about Proverbs 5:9–10, another context in which the wisdom teacher was warning against sexual sin, "Lest you give your honor to others and your years to the merciless, lest strangers take their fill of your strength, and your labors go to the house of a foreigner." Many people reading these words know persons who have become involved in an illicit affair, and the consequence was that they forfeited a faithful spouse and a lovely home. They hurt impressionable children and lost caring friends, all for the sake of a few minutes of pleasure. Sexual sin *always* leads to harm.

No one has ever come to me, a pastor and Bible professor, to extol the joys of an illicit sexual relationship. But they have come to me wounded and hurting, having been caught in the undertow of impurity. They had thought the grass was greener on the other side of the street, but instead of finding bliss, they inflicted pain on themselves, their families, their friends, and their church. They learned too late the truth of God's wisdom for living well: "He who does it destroys himself."

As you read Proverbs 5:11, what comes to mind? "And at the end of your life you groan, when your flesh and body are consumed." That verse concerns the physical suffering that results from physical sin. Long ago, God inspired wisdom writers to record that we will suffer physically if we involve ourselves in sexual sin. So many people today are suffering physically because they engaged in sexual behavior that the Bible calls sinful. Physical sin leads to physical suffering. Other painful circumstances are shame, unwanted pregnancies, and deception to cover up the sin.

God's word affirms the harm of sexual sin. Whenever we face temptation, we should repeat to ourselves the truth of God's word—sexual sin will bring harm. When men talk with me about this issue, I tell them to remember and repeat the five Ps. These are affirmations of the harm of sexual sin.[1] First, when tempted, say, "*My prayer life* will be ruined." Psalm 66:18 says, "If I had cherished iniquity in my heart, the LORD would not have listened." We cannot have a meaningful prayer life if we entertain sinful thoughts. We'll lose all intimacy with God. We'll lose the power and comfort of the Holy Spirit. That's a consequence of sexual sin, even if the sin is only mental.

Second, say, "*My purity* will be spoiled." Our moral integrity and spiritual power are dependent on maintaining a life of purity. If we lose our purity, we lose all integrity. Our prayer life will be ruined, and our purity spoiled.

Third, when tempted, if you're married, say, "*My passion for my spouse* will be diminished." Sexual sin, in deed or thought, compromises intimacy with a spouse, both emotionally and physically. Sexual sin has profoundly negative effects on a marriage.

Fourth, when facing temptation, say, "Important *people will be hurt*." We all have a circle of influence. People are looking at us. Our children are looking at us, our grandchildren, friends, neighbors, and brothers and sisters in Christ. Sexual sin always, always hurts all of those people. Remember the people who will be hurt, and don't hurt them.

Fifth, say, "I will experience *pain*." The momentary pleasure of sin is far outweighed by its short-term and long-term pain. What did Proverbs 6:32–33 say? "He who commits adultery lacks sense; he who does it destroys himself. He will get wounds and dishonor, and his disgrace will not be wiped away."

When facing sexual temptation, remember and repeat the five P's—your prayer life, your purity, your passion for your spouse, the people who'll be hurt, and the pain you'll experience.

God's way makes as much sense today as it ever did. Following God's way is not only physically healthy, it's also emotionally and spiritually healthy. Don't be a simpleton. Be wise. Listen to God's wisdom, heed his warnings, and live by his counsel.

What if you've already fallen prey to sexual temptation? Confess it as sin, receive God's forgiveness and cleansing, and return to a lifestyle of purity. God is ready to forgive, and his church is ready to help you and hold you accountable. Are you ready to confess and repent?

If you are involved in an affair, or some sort of impurity, get out now before you bring even greater shame to your God, and greater pain in your life and in the lives of other people. Purity is the only way to please God and enjoy a happy and healthy life. Choose God's way, for your family, for yourself, and for the glory of God in your life. Heed God's wisdom for living well.

QUESTIONS FOR
REFLECTION

1. In what ways do you think the contemporary church is being affected by the sexual messages and practices common in Western culture? How are you and your friends affected?

2. What attitudes or behaviors are important in marriage in order to prevent even the desire for extramarital sexual activity?

3. What are some examples of the use of isolation, beauty, flattery, and a flirtatious look that are influencing people toward sexual activity outside marriage?

4. What specific actions can you take to "keep your heart with all vigilance" (Prov 4:23) so that you will win the war being waged in your mind?

5. Try memorizing and repeating "the five P's" that affirm the harm of sexual sin.

CONCLUSION

A high school teacher of mine sometimes spoke to her students about how to live after graduation as educated people. One statement she repeated to us was this: "Education is not knowing all the answers; it's knowing where to find the answers." I remember thinking that was a strange statement. I wanted to know all the answers, and I thought the more answers I knew, the more educated I would be. However, she had been alive much longer than me. Years later, the truth of what she had said began to dawn on me. Over the years I have learned more and more, and I have forgotten more and more. But when I remember where I learned something, I can go to the source and recall the facts when I need them. In this book you have encountered quite a bit of truth. Unless you have a truly rare ability to retain information, you will forget a lot of what you have read. I hope you will not forget the source of the truth. To paraphrase my high school teacher, living well is not knowing all the answers; it's knowing where to find the answers.

Having read this book, you know where to find the answers to living well. We don't look to the messages droned nonstop by the media, we don't fall in line with a corrupt culture, and we don't even live by the advice of friends. We go to God's book of wisdom. He ordered the universe, he made us, and he gave us his truth for living in his world. Is he wise? He is God. He is the source of all wisdom, so only he can make us wise. In reading this book you have accessed God's wisdom. But what if you forget? You know where to find the answers, so go back to his book of wisdom, again and again. Saturate your mind with God's truth. Make his wisdom yours. You *will* find out how great life can be. With the help of God's Spirit, you can live well.

NOTES

Preface

1. A. J. Jacobs, *The Know-It-All: One Man's Humble Quest to Become the Smartest Person in the World* (New York: Simon & Schuster, 2004).
2. Gilbert K. Chesterton, *Heretics/Orthodoxy* (Nashville: Thomas Nelson, 2000), 169.

Introducing the Book of Proverbs

1. Benjamin Franklin, *Poor Richard's Quotations: Being a Collection of Quotations from Poor Richard Almanacks* (Boulder, CO: Blue Mountain Arts, 1975), 21, 29, 76.
2. Mark Twain, "Memoranda by Mark Twain," *The Galaxy*, July 1870, page 138. Found on http://quoteinvestigator.com/2013/01/17/put-off/.
3. For a description of how the biblical worldview differs from the ideologies of the postmodern West, see N. Allan Moseley, *Thinking Against the Grain: Developing a Biblical Worldview in a Culture of Myths* (Grand Rapids: Kregel, 2003).
4. For an excellent, extended discussion of how the book of Proverbs points to Christ and is fulfilled in him, see Jonathan Akin, *Preaching Christ from Proverbs* (Spring Hill, TN: Rainer Publishing, 2014).
5. William McKane, *Proverbs: A New Approach*, The Old Testament Library (Philadelphia: The Westminster Press, 1970), 276.

6. Derek Kidner, *An Introduction to Wisdom Literature: The Wisdom of Proverbs, Job, and Ecclesiastes* (Downers Grove, IL: InterVarsity Press, 1985), 19.

7. Ted A. Hildebrandt, "Proverb," in *Cracking Old Testament Codes: A Guide to Interpreting the Literary Genres of the Old Testament* (Nashville: Broadman and Holman, 1995), 234.

8. Cited by Roy B. Zuck, *Learning from the Sages: Selected Studies on the Book of Proverbs* (Grand Rapids: Baker Books, 1995), 15.

CHAPTER 1: PEOPLE SKILLS

1. James L. Crenshaw, *Education in Ancient Israel: Across the Deadening Silence* (New York: Doubleday, 1998), 230–33.

CHAPTER 2: OUR POWERFUL WORDS

1. Mary Ann Bird, "A Genius for Loving," *Guideposts Magazine*, January 1985, 29.

2. Michael A. Rousell, *Sudden Influence: How Spontaneous Events Shape Our Lives* (Westport, CT: Praeger Publishers, 2007), 2–3, 26.

3. Quoted in Miller Caldwell, *Have You Seen My ... umm ... Memory?* (Hertford, UK: Authors Online Ltd., 2004), 9.

4. "Mary Kay Ash: Mary Kay Cosmetics," *The Journal of Business Leadership* 1 (1988). Reproduced on http://anbhf.org/laureates/mary-kay-ash/, and article title provided on http://smallbusiness.chron.com/mary-kay-organizational-structure-15525.html, accessed January 16, 2017.

5. Keith Manuel, "Alive because someone listened," *Baptist Press*, February 5, 2008, http://www.baptistpress.com/27340/alive-because-someone-listened.

6. This is a traditional rhyme published in many sources as early as the late 19th century. The author is unknown.

7. Horatio Richmond Palmer, "Angry Words," *Blue Letter Bible*, accessed February 5, 2016, https://www.blueletterbible .org/hymns/a/Angry_Words.cfm.

CHAPTER 3: GOD'S WISDOM FOR WOMEN

1. Brenda Hunter, "The Value of Motherhood," *Where Have All the Mothers Gone?* (Grand Rapids: Zondervan, 1982), 3.

2. Judith Warner, *Perfect Madness: Motherhood in the Age of Anxiety* (New York: Penguin Group, 2006).

3. "Mom's Work Matters: The Many Jobs of a Mother's Day," Salary.com, accessed September 29, 2009, http:// salary.com/personal/layoutscripts/ psnl_articles.asp?tab=psn&cat=cat011&ser=ser031&part=par1450.

Chapter 4: God's Wisdom for Men

1. Meg Meeker, *Strong Fathers, Strong Daughters: 10 Secrets Every Father Should Know* (Washington: Regnery Publishing, 2006), 4.
2. "Court quashes dad's grounding of 12-year-old daughter," *CBC News*, June 19, 2008, http://www.cbc.ca/news/canada/court-quashes-dad-s-grounding-of-12-year-old-daughter-1.717665.
3. Katherine Kersten, "Spank kids and lose them to the overzealous government," *Minneapolis Star Tribune*, December 2, 2007, http://www.startribune.com/local/12043206.html.

Chapter 5: The Foolishness of Anger

1. Golda Meir, "Selected Quotes from Golda Meir ," *Golda Meir Center for Political Leadership* at Metropolitan State College of Denver, accessed January 5, 2017, http://www.msudenver.edu/golda/goldameir/golda-quotes/.
2. I first began to see how these verses can be applied to the development of anger when I read Adrian Rogers, *God's Way to Health, Wealth, and Wisdom* (Nashville: Broadman Press, 1987), 108–10.
3. Tertullian, "On Prayer," in *The Ante-Nicene Fathers*, ed. Alexander Roberts and James Donaldson (Peabody, MA: Hendrickson Publishers, 2004), 3.685.
4. Hermas, "The Pastor," in *The Ante-Nicene Fathers*, ed. Alexander Roberts and James Donaldson (Peabody, MA: Hendrickson Publishers, 2004), 2:23–24.

Chapter 6: The Strange Disease of Pride

1. Christopher Rocchio and Steve Rogers, "American Idol's Seventh Season Debuts Huge but Ratings Dip a Bit," *Reality TV World*, January 16, 2008, www.realitytvworld.com/news/american-idol-seventh-season-debuts%20-huge-but-ratings-dip-bit-6401.php
2. Eric Walsh, "Factbox–'American Idol' still most-watched U.S. TV show," *Reuters*, May 16, 2009, www.reuters.com/article/PBLSHG/idUSN1528950320090517.
3. Isaac Watts, "When I Survey the Wondrous Cross," *The Hymnal for Worship and Celebration* (Nashville: Word, 1986), 185.

Chapter 7: Holiness, Happiness, and Health

1. Andrew Clark and Orsolya Lelkes, "Deliver Us from Evil: Religion as Insurance," 2005, accessed January 9, 2017, https://halshs.archives-ouvertes.fr/halshs-00590570/document.

2. Robert Ornstein and David Sobel, *Healthy Pleasures* (Woburn, MA: Perseus Books, 1989), 4–5.

3. Harold G. Koenig, *Medicine, Religion, and Health: Where Science and Spirituality Meet* (West Conshohocken, PA: Templeton Press, 2008), 53.

4. Quoted by Jane Manner in *The Silver Treasury: Prose and Poetry for Every Mood* (London: S. French, Ltd., 1934), 323–24.

5. Francis Brown, S. R. Driver, and Charles A. Briggs, "*gehah,*" *The Brown-Driver-Briggs Hebrew and English Lexicon* (Peabody, MA: Hendrickson Publishers, 2006), 155.

Chapter 8: Dollars and Sense

1. Robert Frank, "Marrying for Love...of Money," *The Wall Street Journal*, December 14, 2007, accessed January 18, 2017. Viewed at https://biz.yahoo.com/wallstreet/071214/sb119760031991928727_id.html?.v=1.

Chapter 9: Work: "A Very Sacred Matter"

1. Robert Frost, "Michael Moncur's (Cynical) Quotations," *The Quotations Page*, accessed January 18, 2017, viewed at http://www.quotationspage.com/quote/808.html.

2. Nathan O. Hatch, "The Perils of Being a Professional," *Christianity Today*, November 11, 1991, 26.

3. Cited by W. R. Forrester in *Christian Vocation: Studies in Faith and Work* (New York: Charles Scribner's Sons, 1953), 148.

4. Ewald M. Plass, ed., *What Luther Says: An Anthology* (St. Louis: Concordia Publishing House, 1959), 3:1493.

5. Hatch, "The Perils of Being a Professional," 27.

Chapter 10: Seduction of a Simpleton

1. Randy C. Alcorn, *Christians in the Wake of the Sexual Revolution: Recovering Our Sexual Sanity* (Portland: Multnomah, 1985), 31.

2. William Frey, "Really Good Sex," *Christianity Today*, August 19, 1991, 12.

3. Charles Swindoll, *Three Steps Forward, Two Steps Back: Persevering Through Pressure* (Nashville: Thomas Nelson Publishers, 1980), 100–1.

4. I also included this list in *Thinking Against the Grain: Developing a Biblical Worldview in a Culture of Myths* (Grand Rapids: Kregel, 2003), 181–82.

SCRIPTURE INDEX

Old Testament

New Testament

TRUTHFORLIFE®

THE BIBLE-TEACHING MINISTRY OF **ALISTAIR BEGG**

The mission of Truth For Life is to teach the Bible with clarity and relevance so that unbelievers will be converted, believers will be established, and local churches will be strengthened.

Daily Program

Each day, Truth For Life distributes the Bible teaching of Alistair Begg across the U.S. and in several locations outside of the U.S. through 1,800 radio outlets. To find a radio station near you, visit **truthforlife.org/stationfinder**.

Free Teaching

The daily program, and Truth For Life's entire teaching archive of over 2,000 Bible-teaching messages, can be accessed for free online and through Truth For Life's full-feature mobile app. Download the free mobile app at **truthforlife.org/app** and listen free online at **truthforlife.org**.

At-Cost Resources

Books and full-length teaching from Alistair Begg on CD, DVD, and USB are available for purchase at cost, with no markup. Visit **truthforlife.org/store**.

Where to Begin?

If you're new to Truth For Life and would like to know where to begin listening and learning, find starting point suggestions at **truthforlife.org/firststep**. For a full list of ways to connect with Truth For Life, visit **truthforlife.org/subscribe**.

Contact Truth For Life

P.O. Box 398000 Cleveland, Ohio 44139
phone 1 (888) 588-7884   **email** letters@truthforlife.org
 /truthforlife   @truthforlife   truthforlife.org